SHORT STORIES FROM THE BRITISH INDIAN ARMY

SHORT STORIES FROM THE BRITISH INDIAN ARMY

by

J Francis

Vij Books India Pvt Ltd

New Delhi (India)

Vij Books India Pvt Ltd
(Publishers, Distributors & Importers)
2/19 (Second Floor), Ansari Road, Darya Ganj
New Delhi - 110002
Phones: 91-11-43596460, 91-11- 65449971
Fax: 91-11-47340674
web: www.vijbooks.com
e-mail : vijbooks@rediffmail.com

ISBN: 978-93-84464-67-7

The views expressed in the book are of the author.

This book is meant for educational and learning purposes, the author of the book has taken all reasonable care to ensure that the contents of the book do not violate any existing copyright or other intellectual property rights of any person in any manner whatsoever. In the event the editor has been unable to track any source and if any copyright has been inadvertently infringed, please notify the publisher in writing for the corrective action.

This Book is dedicated to all those Indian Soldiers who fought and won many battles against heavy odds in the World War I and brought glory and honour to the Indian Army.

CONTENTS

LIST OF ABBREVIATIONS

Brig	Brigadier
BIA	British Indian Army
Capt	Captain
CO	Commanding Officer
COAS	Chief of Army Staff
C in C	Commander in Chief
Col	Colonel
Fd	Field
Gen	General
Govt	Government
Hav	Havaldar
Hony	Honorary
ICO	Indian Commissioned Officer
Jem	Jemadar
KCO	King Commissioned officer
KCIO	King Commissioned Indian Officer
Lt	Lieutenant
Lt Col	Lieutenant Colonel
Lt Gen	Lieutenant General
L/Nk	Lance Naik

Maj Gen	Major General
MC	Military Cross
Nk	Naik
NCO	Non Commissioned Officer
Rfn	Rifleman
2/Lt	Second Lieutenant
VC	Victoria Cross
VCO	Viceroy Commissioned Officer
WW	World War

PRAISE FOR THE BOOK

In his third book on anecdotes primarily centered around feats of gallantry exhibited on the battlefields of World War I and World War II by Indian soldiers of the pre-independence Indian Army (referred to by the author as British Indian Army), Col J Francis has in simple, lucid and graphic style annotated with good maps and appropriate historical references brilliantly portrayed the colossal contribution made by the gallant Indian soldiers and the units of the British Indian Army.

The author has covered a vast canvas of time and geographical locations from 1914 till end of Second World War and included all the theatres of war from France-Flanders, Mesopotamia, Dardanelles to Africa, Palestine-Egypt, Italy and Burma. The battles selected and the description of the sacrifices made by Indian soldiers that contributed significantly to the successful outcome and/ or enhanced the prestige of the Indian Army units are indeed immensely captivating and should contribute towards motivating the youth of the country towards taking up Army as a career.

The book is also a great addition to the military-historical archive of the Indian Army and an excellent reference book in Unit and formation libraries.

Lt Gen S Pattabhiraman (Retd), PVSM,AVSM,SM,VSM

Former VCOAS and Western Army Commander

****

'Short Stories of the British Indian Army (BIA)' written by Col J Francis is an excellent endeavour to highlight the valour and sacrifice of the Indian soldiers while fighting abroad. Painstaking research must have been undertaken by the author to find out the details of each episode of valour and the human angle of the brave heart, like his photograph, place of birth, family, village and how he is being remembered in the present times. These small anecdotes make the Book very easy and interesting read.

The effort in the World War I by the Indian Soldiers was indeed substantial. Besides, the deployments abroad, exposed our troops to the living standards existing abroad, especially that of Europe. On return, these soldiers assisted the society to improve their lot, within the means and resources available. The idea of an egalitarian society, freedom, justice and all round prosperity was advocated by them, similar to what they had experienced during the tenures abroad. These ideas strengthened the nascent independence movement in the domestic political arena.

The author has described the battles in great detail, where valour and bravery was recognized. The language used is simple and can be understood by even a non-military person. The students of military history will find this book a handy reference which gives out names, dates, units participated etc in one small handbook. It can, therefore, be termed as a 'reference handbook'.

I wish the author could have also given an 'Index' at the end of the book, for easy cross reference. Though, the book is well laid out in chapters and sub-chapters, an 'index' would have been an invaluable help to a researcher.

It is heartening to know that the book has been translated in to Hindi, also. The book will and should get wider readership, beyond the military. It will certainly enthuse the youth to join the Armed Forces and the young soldiers to emulate the brave actions of their forefathers.

Lt Gen Milan Naidu PVSM,AVSM,YSM (Retd).

Former VCOAS, Army Commander ARTRAC, Member Armed Forces Tribunel.

****

My compliments to Col J Francis for a beautiful and meaningful way of paying tribute to the heroes of the Indian Army. This book is much more than history, it is about the actions of gallant officers and men, their indomitable spirit, unmatched bravery and above all their sacrifices for the Nation.

The stories portray the incredible courage, supreme sacrifice and valour of Indian soldiers led by young dynamic leaders. The inspirational sketches of extraordinarily brave young officers and soldiers who converted highly adverse operational situations into victory highlights the professional commitment and ethos of the Indian Army.

Am sanguine the book will rekindle the interest of all who wear olive green or have donned them in the past. For the young officer, its a treasure trove full of inspiration. In fact, it needs to be read by all citizens to appreciate and feel proud of the spirit of sacrifice that's ingrained in every soldier of this Great Army.

Jai Hind

Lt General Raymond Joseph Noronha, AVSM, SM.

****

I had served as a Senior Instructor (Air) at the Defence Services Staff College Wellington for two years during 80s, besides being a serious student of Military History. Familiarity and knowledge with Military History has equipped us with certain understanding to comprehend the historical analysis in its correct perspective. After going through the stories in the book, SHORT STORIES FROM THE BRITISH INDIAN ARMY written by Col Francis, I found that some of them I was reading for the first time and were refreshing to be proud of our History, our Regiments and most of all our Brave men who brought distinction and dignity to our Nation with their Skill with innovative spirit.

According to this chronicle about 87,000 Indian soldiers were killed and nearly equal number was wounded. Over 4800 gallantry awards including 31 Victoria Cross were given. The Short Stories compiled here speak eloquently of the bravery and dedication of the Indian Soldiers who were pitted against more advanced armies of the Axis power countries. At the end of the WW II when the Indian Army returned home, the freedom struggle was going on. Despite the apolitical nature of our Armed Forces, possibly British were apprehensive if these committed soldiers would combine with aggressive politics in achieving the goal and that is a Free India. This view of the author is not well articulated in any written document that came my way so far. But is not farfetched and appears logical.

These stories reflect passion, valor and bravery of our brave men who sacrificed lives for their Nation, irrespective that we were not Free then but yet they represented the Spirit of India. Overall the stories are written in simple format, easy to understand and the effort is worthy of appreciation.

Finally Wishing Col Francis a Happy Readership and to the Readers a good Ride through the Brave journey of our talented Men and Officers of the Indian Army, whose every action is worthy of Emulation.

Air Vice Marshal Hamid Shahul, AVSM,VSM (Retd)

Former Chairman, Airport Authority of India.

****

In his third book, related to the Élan and Achievements of the Indian Soldiers, Colonel Francis has started from the very origin of the present day institution of the Indian Army. In his first book he had narrated 29 stories of 'Game Changing Events' of the wars and conflict situations faced by India, since independence, giving their overall importance to the ongoing operations in particular and to the safe guarding of the Integrity of our Nation in general and how the contribution made by those 'Extra Ordinary Soldiers' in achieving victory in those fateful events.

Based on the feedback of the readers of the first book, in his second book, he widened the spectrum. In addition to some more events related to war, he spelled out the very significant contribution of the Indian Army in the consolidation of the Indian Union, post-Independence. Its development into a modern, potent and powerful instrument of the State, and its achievements as well as those of its appendage organisations such as Rashtriya Rifles, NSG and NCC, in the fields of sports & adventure activities. Also included in that book were some very inspiring life sketches of some exceptionally brave and determined officers and the emergence of Indian Army's 'Women Power'

In this book the author has again retained highlighting of the extra ordinary bravery, steadfastness, camaraderie, self-sacrifice and above all loyalty of the Indian soldier to the Government, the Institution i.e. the Army and the Unit, as the central thread of the stories. He, in this book, has covered a vast expanse in time and space. From the origin of the Army, he takes the reader to almost the whole of the world and through the changing mode of warfare and highlights the sterling performance of the Indian soldier: Warriors Par Excellence, in the guarding as well as expansion of the British Empire.

Retaining his gripping 'Short Story Style' of narration, Francis first gives the 'Overall Backdrop' and thereafter the 'Run-up' to the event followed by the 'Ring Side' commentary of the 'Act'. The events included in the book have been so done with great care. I dare say that even for very avid readers of the history of the Indian Army, this book has something new and important and hence it is a priceless treasure of information. Francis has really dived deep to pull out this gem.

Major General SP Kapoor, VSM (Retd).

Former General Officer Commanding of a Division and Member State Consumer Commission.

****

Col Francis has put together a marvelous collection of stories of heroism. His narrative is so lucid and vivid that one can actually imagine the battle unfold in front of the eyes and smell the gun powder.

My eyes were wet after I finished reading the Last stand at Saragarhi. One can only stand and salute those men of steel who gave up their today for our tomorrow.

I sincerely recommend this book to anyone who is looking for a source of inspiration. This is really a masterpiece and a tonic for the mind.

Major General (Dr) Manmohan Singh, VSM, MS, MCh.
MG medical Western Command

****

'Short Stories from the British Indian Army' is precisely what its title indicates. Colonel J Francis has selected 26 short stories to bring out the contribution made by the gallant Indian Soldiers and their Units under the British. The canvas covers 167 pages diligently researched work encompassing a time frame from 1897 to 1947 on the valiant action of Indian soldiers under British. The well documented book is not a serious study of history but a good compilation of battle stories and account of heroics of brave Indian soldiers.

The Chapter on Indian officers outlines the early inception of Indians as officers and Indianisation of British Indian Army. The book concludes with a narrative on the life and contribution of one of the finest British Indian Officer World War II produced, Field Marshal Slim.

The book is a must read for all budding young men who wants to know about Indian Army and its past.

Brig Umar Farook A, VSM
Chief Signal Officer
HQ ATNK&K Area

****

PREFACE

The British Crown took over the control of the three Presidency Armies in India in the year 1858. This Army was informally called 'Indian Army'. Lord Kitchener was the C in C from 1902 to 1909. He amalgamated the erstwhile three Presidency Armies and grouped them into brigades and divisions.

For the sake of clarity, the then Indian Army is referred to as the British Indian Army (BIA) in this book. It consisted of units with Indian men, Indian Viceroy Commissioned Officers (VCO) and British King Commissioned Officers (KCO). In 1919, Kodandera Madappa Cariappa and a few other Indians were commissioned for the first time as King Commission Indian Officers (KCIO) in BIA.

British Army units stationed in India were known as the British Army in India. The Army of the Princely States in India was known as the Imperial Service Troops. Typically a brigade comprised one/two BIA battalions and one/two British Army infantry battalions. The role of BIA was to protect and expand the territory of British India. They were also responsible to assist the civil police force when needed.

The British were apprehensive of the expansion of the Russian influence outside their country and of it spilling over through Afghanistan into India. They wanted to have control over the affairs of Afghanistan. However, in spite of three major wars, Afghanistan could not be subjugated. The Pathans remained a formidable enemy of British Government. Therefore, most of the Army Cantonments in India were located closer to Afghanistan border in and around the present day North West Pakistan (Waziristan). Meerut, Lucknow, Mhow, Secunderabad and Bangalore were the other major cantonments in India.

Besides ongoing battles in the NW Frontiers, BIA participated in major wars outside India; in the Boxer Rebellion in 1900 in China, WW I and WW II in Europe, Africa, Middle East and South East Asian Countries. The first and the most incredible story in this Book is that of the Battle of Saragarhi. Amongst many battles fought against Afghans, the Battle at Saragarhi in 1897 stands out prominently. The conduct of the 21 Indian soldiers in that Battle has no parallel in the history of warfare.

In 1900, Indian Army units were moved to China and were deployed in Beijing to break the 55 days old siege by the Boxers (Chinese radicals). BIA successfully broke the siege by crawling through the sewage canals and saved 400 foreigners from their death. This successful story is also mentioned in Chinese history.

The first Total War or Global War (also known as the Great War until 1939) was fought between Allies (led by the United Kingdom) and the Central Power (led by Germany) in Europe, Africa, Palestine and Mesopotamia between 1914 and 1918. Later in 1939, this War was renamed as WW I. The causes of this War are the end results of long and complex political, economic and military related conflict of interests amongst European Nations. (The details are not relevant to this Book hence not included.)

BIA entered and fought this War on behalf of the United Kingdom against the Central Power. BIA units which were sent to Europe and Africa were known as Indian Expeditionary Forces (IEF). Seven such Forces designated as IEF 'A to G' were sent from India to various theatres of War. It was with the approval and financial support of Indian political leaders and heads of Princely States in India that Indians were sent to fight the war outside India with the hope that the ongoing freedom movement would be considered favorably by the British Government once the War ended.

IEF 'A' was inducted to reinforce the British Army in Europe at the Western Front. The Western Front, which stretched nearly for 400 miles from North Sea to Switzerland, was the scene of major battles at Ypres, Somme, Verdun and Cambrai. In their effort to prevent the German Army from reaching the Atlantic sea coast, the British Army had suffered heavy casualties especially at Ypres within a few weeks of the start of the War.

Indian troops were moved to Ypres, which is located at the northern end of the Western Front in Belgium. This IEF was not adequately trained for large scale trench warfare which was being fought along the Western Front. Their weapons, equipment and clothing were unsuitable for the climatic conditions obtained there. For the first time new generation of .303 bore magazine fed rifles were issued to the Indian troops along with two machine guns to a battalion just before they were inducted into the battle.

Much of the combat was in the form of mass attack in waves across the no man's land against row of well fortified trenches created in depth. The attacks progressed very slowly. The defenders inflicted heavy causalities from well fortified trenches in each engagement. Under these conditions, which were new to Indian soldiers, they acquitted themselves creditably and contributed to the prevention of 'German Race to the Sea' and ultimate victory of Allies in WW I.

For the first time Indian soldiers were awarded the Victoria Cross in recognition of their bravery and dedication during this War. The first recipients were Darwan Singh Negi and Khudadad Khan. Many other awards and Battle Honors were also given to the Indian soldiers in the Western Front.

During the First World War, the Allies had opened a Second Front in Turkey (Gallipoli) to draw out the German pressure from the Western Front. IEF 'G' was sent to Gallipoli. IEF 'B' and 'C' were sent to Africa to capture the colonies of Central Power. IEF 'D', 'E' and 'F' participated in this War at Mesopotamia, Palestine and Suez Canal Area respectively.

During the course of this War between 1914 and 1918, many new weapon systems and tactics were introduced. Infantry formations were reorganized. By the end of this War the trench warfare was fought at section and platoon levels with 10 men in a section under the command of a NCO.

Deadly weapons such as poison gas, flame throwers and high explosive grenades were added during the course of this War. Wireless sets provided communication in mobile battles. Tanks were used in both defensive and offensive roles. Artillery guns brought down fixed and moving barrages from longer distances unknown before this War. Aircrafts were used as fighters and bombers in small numbers. This form of warfare was new to Indian soldiers and they were witness to the gradual evolution in modern war.

More than 70,000 Indians were killed and equal numbers were wounded in battle. Indian Army units were awarded 74 Battle Honors from all the theatres of War between 1914 and 1918. For individual bravery, seven Indian soldiers were decorated with the Victoria Cross (VC) which is the highest and most prestigious award for gallantry in the face of the enemy for most conspicuous bravery, or some daring or pre-eminent act of valor or self-sacrifice, or extreme devotion to duty.

The third Afghan War was fought in 1919. It was a short war started by the Afghans. The British Indian Army thwarted the offensive and used air power to bomb Kabul and other towns. The king of Afghanistan, Amanullah Khan sued for peace and concluded a treaty restoring peace with India. One VC was awarded for bravery to an Indian Sepoy in this war. During the next decade, the Indian Army remained engaged with the rebels in Waziristan while undergoing many organizational changes.

For the first time in 1919, Indians were given King Commission and the first batch of Indian officers was posted to selected Regiments of Indian Army units. They were known as King Commissioned Indian Officers. Subsequently, the Indian Military Academy (IMA) was established 1932 at Dehradun. Those who passed out from there were known as Indian Commissioned officers.

The Defense Services Staff College (DSSC) was raised at Quetta (now in Pakistan) and a large number of Indian and British officers were trained in staff duties and prepared them for higher ranks. (DSSC was later moved to Wellington, Nilgiris in India.)

In the Second World War (WW II), the Allies once again fought against the Axis Powers between 1939 and 1945. Nazi Germany and her allies; this time Japan and Italy, had become powerful and began annexing the neighboring countries to unite all German-speaking people under one country in Europe. Poland was attacked by Germany on 1 September 1939. Two days later, Britain declared war against Germany.

BIA once again entered the war to fight on behalf of Great Britain. While BIA fought for Britain against the Germans and Italians in Europe East and North Africa, they faced the formidable Japanese Army which was part of the Axis Forces at the Eastern Frontiers of India in Burma and Malaya.

The major operations in which British Indian Army units and formations participated in Africa in WW II were at the Battle of Keren in Eretria, operations Battle Axe, Crusader, First and Second Battles of

El Alamein. BIA units also fought against pro German, Syrian and Iraqi forces in Northern Syria successfully under Major General Slim (later Field Marshal). This prevented the Germans using Syria as a launching pad to Africa.

In Italy, battles were fought right across the country from the southern tip after crossing Sicily, to the German Borders with Italy in the north against series of Defense lines. As many as four Indian Divisions and an Independent Brigade of BIA were involved in the Italian campaign. They crossed Sangro River and advanced deep into Italy. After the battle of Monte Cassino in 1945, BIA Units participated in the battle of Senio before the Germans surrendered on 29 April 1945.

A major part of 14th Army in Burma was manned by Indians. They fought both during the defeat in the beginning and victory towards the end. Important battles in Burma Campaign were fought at Arakan in the Battle of Admin Box, Kohima, Imphal, Meiktila, Mandalay in Central Burma, and at Akyab and Rangoon. The victory at Kohima and Imphal was the turning point in the War in Burma.

When WW II began in 1939, the strength of BIA was about 200,000. The strength rose to 2.5 million, more than tenfold in August 1945 at the culmination of WW II. BIA was not fully prepared to join the WW II in 1939 as it was not expected to get involved in the fight against the Axis Forces at that time. More Indians were enrolled and trained during the War.

About 87,000 Indian soldiers were killed and nearly equal number wounded. Over 4800 gallantry awards including 31 VCs were given to Indian soldiers. The Indian Army won many laurels for their bravery and dedication. At the end of the WW II when the Indian Army returned home, the freedom struggle was in full swing. Having witnessed the performance of the formidable Indian rank and file in the recently concluded War, the British realized that subjugating Indians in the future would be impossible. This speeded up their decision to free India from the British rule. The Nation was eagerly waiting for independence which was ultimately achieved on 15 August 1947. With the partition of the country into India and Pakistan, the British Indian Army was also divided into Indian Army and Pakistan Army. Thus the true Indian Army was born along with the freedom on the 15th of August 1947.

In this Book, an attempt has been made to bring forth the memory of those brave heroes, who have done proud to the community of Indian soldiers by their bravery and loyalty to their units and sacrifices they had made whenever it was demanded and wherever they were taken. The Short Stories presented in this Book speaks eloquently of the bravery and dedication of the Indian Soldiers who were pitted against more advanced armies of the Axis power countries.

It is appropriate that we remember them during this centenary year of WW I. I salute them and dedicate this Book in their memory.

- Author

ACKNOWLEDGEMENT

I realize that a Book of this nature requires very extensive and intensive research. I could not have done this without the support of my well wishers and friends. I thank them for their unreserved support. I thank my wife, daughter and son for their contribution in completing the Book so as to be able to publish during this year of Centenary of World War I. Many of my senior colleagues patiently read the draft and gave many valuable suggestions. I thank them for their valuable inputs. My special thanks to Maj Gen SP Kapoor, VSM for his untiring effort in translating this book in Hindi and giving his valuable opinion. Most of all I thank Brigadier PK Vij of the Vij Books India Pvt Ltd who has been instrumental in releasing the Book in time.

- Author

LAST STAND AT SARAGARHI

O God, give me these boons
that never shall I shirk from doing good deeds
that never shall I fear when I go into battle
and that with surety I shall attain victory.

- Sri Guru Govind Singhji

Saragarhi was one of the eleven Forts on the Samana Ranges located in the erstwhile North Western Frontier Province of British India, now part of Kohat District of Khyber Pakhtunkhwa Province in Pakistan. This area falls south of the strategically important Khyber Pass and the city of Peshawar. (Khyber Pass is located on the Durant Line which is the border between Pakistan and Afghanistan). It was one of the most difficult areas to rule by the British. Many battles were fought in this area. It will not be an exaggeration to say that every stone in Khyber has been soaked in blood. The Afridi and Orakzais of the Pashtun tribes inhabited the Valley on both sides of the Samana Ranges.

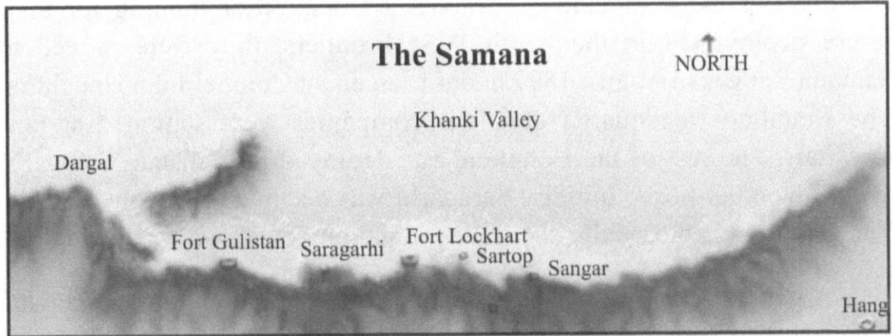

Skyline of the Samana Ranges

Maharaja Ranjit Singh during his reign over this region constructed many forts on the Samana Ranges to locate his Army in this trouble prone area. Later when the British annexed the Punjab in 1849, they took over this area as well. They renovated the existing forts and added a few more to provide protection to their garrison. The main forts were Dargai, Gulistan and Lockhart. The distance between Gulistan and Lockhart is about eight kms. Saragarhi, which is located midway was an abandoned fort near a small village, was reoccupied in 1897 as an intermediate post to relay heliographic (method of sending message by Morse code with the use of reflected sun light by a mirror) messages between Forts Gulistan and Lockhart which were not inter-visible.

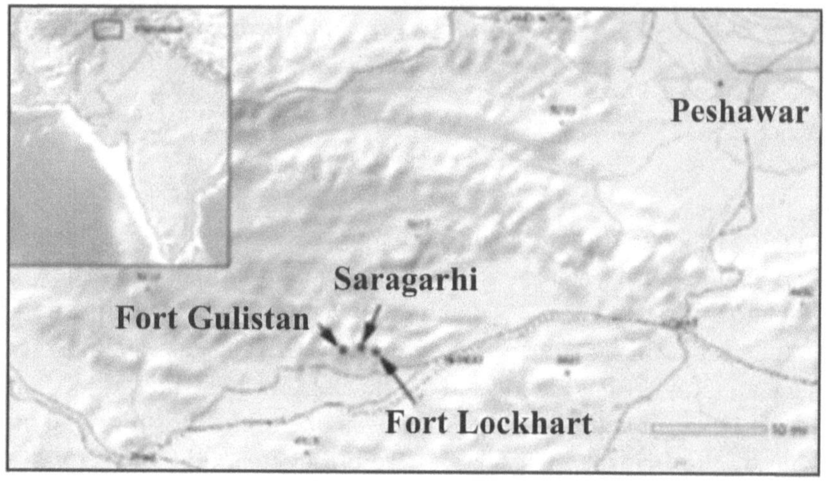

Map of Samna Range

On 20 April 1894, the 36th Sikh Regiment (Now 4 SIKH) was raised under the command of Colonel J Cook. After training for their future deployment in the North West Frontiers, they were moved to Samana Ranges in August 1897 under Lieutenant Colonel John Haughton. The Battalion Headquarter and four companies were stationed at Fort Lockhart. The rest of the Battalion was deployed in Gulistan, Saragarhi and a few other posts. Initially Saragarhi was occupied by about 10 men. The Battalion had partially succeeded in gaining control over this region.

A general uprising by the Afghans began on either side of Samana Ranges in 1897 against the British. In August and September, the Pashtuns made many attempts to capture the Forts on the Samana Ranges. Their attempts were frustrated by the 36th Sikh with heavy casualty on the attackers. On 3 September a group of Afridi tribes launched a massive attack on Fort Gulistan. This was repulsed. Considering the constant threat posed to Fort Gulistan, it was reinforced with troops from Lockhart.

As was expected, the Pashtuns attacked Gulistan on 11 September. Once again the Sikhs prevailed over the Pashtuns. After having defeated the insurgents, the relief column which came from Fort Lockhart returned to Lockhart. On their way back, they left another 10 men at Saragrhi relaying post to make it stronger against the expected hostile action by the Pashtuns. Thus on 11 September Saragarhi was held by one NCO and 20 Sepoys of 36 Sikh. Havaldar Ishar Singh was the commander. The Saragarhi defense consisted of a small square stone block house and a relaying post with good view to Lockhart and Gulistan. The area around the post had boulders and dry shrubs.

Around 0900 hrs on12 September 1897, Saragarhi was attacked by hundreds of Afridi and Orakzai tribesmen. Sepoy Gurmukh Singh was the signaler. Lt Col Haughton was watching and reading the signal sent by Gurmukh Singh from Lockhart. The initial attack was repulsed with heavy casualty on the attacker. During the second assault, ten men of 36 Sikh were killed and a few seriously wounded. A message from Lockhart was received stating that they could spot thousands of Pashtuns surrounding Saragarhi and therefore they could not send any reinforcement. Ishar Singh, knowing full well what was in store for him and his men, reorganized the defenses to face the attackers who were climbing up towards the Post in large numbers.

The attackers closed in with the Post and demolished one corner of the wall. There was a fierce hand-to-hand fight. The leader of the attacking group asked the Sikhs to surrender. Ishar Singh refused and kept on fighting in spite of his serious injury. There were nine Sikhs still left alive. They fixed their bayonets and were ready to do what was expected of them. A large number of attackers were killed in the hand-to-hand fight. The attackers set the Post on fire with dry shrubs thrown into the building. The Sikhs came out and faced the murderous assault of the attackers until all twenty of them were killed. The entire sequence of the battle was signaled to Lockhart as it occurred by the only surviving Sikh; Sepoy Gumukh Singh, the signaler.

Now it was Gurmukh Singh's turn to avenge the death of his comrades. Though he was alone against many hundred, this brave Sepoy decided to follow the example set by Hav Ishar Singh. He asked for permission from his Company Commander to close down the communication and fight the insurgents. The contents of his last message read as "People say one's brothers are like one's own arms. If you were our brothers, you would have seen our plight and helped us with ammunition. But it was beyond your power: the enemy has blocked all the roads. Brothers, we have served our Guru and our Emperor and now we take leave of you forever." The permission was flashed back from Fort Lockhart. Later his dead body was found among the 21 men of 36 Sikh, who had laid down their life fighting; the last man last round. The Fort was lost to the rebels on that day. More than 600 dead bodies of Pasthuns were counted around the fort after it was later recaptured.

Demolished Fort Saragarhi

Thus ended an incomparable saga of bravery and self sacrifice of 21 Indian Soldiers. All 21 who had preferred to die honorably in battle rather than surrendering to their enemy were decorated with Indian Order of Merit, the highest bravery award eligible to an Indian soldier at that time. Their dependents were given 50 acres of land and Rs 500 each. The last stand taken by the 21 men of 36 Sikh in the Battle at Saragarhi was reported to the Queen of England; the first ever such report. When the statement of this heroic deed was read in the British Parliament in London, all the members of the parliament stood up and gave a standing ovation, a unique event in the history of British Parliament.

Saragarhi Day is celebrated on 12 September every year in memory of the 21 Martyrs. Many memorials and two Gurudwars, one each at Amritsar and Ferozpur, have been dedicated to the heroes of Saragarhi. The Battle at Saragarhi is one of eight stories of collective bravery published by United Nations Educational, Scientific and Cultural Organization. It has been mentioned as one of the five most significant events of its kind in the world which includes the Battle of Thermopylae associated with the heroic stand of a small Greek force against the Persian Army of Xerxes I in 480 B.C.

MAP – EUROPE DURING WORLD WAR I

FIRST INDIAN VC - WESTERN FRONT

The British Indian Army (BIA) was reorganized on the lines of British Army in Divisions and Brigades between 1902 and 1909 under the Kitchener Reforms. Large number of units of the BIA was deployed in the NW Frontiers areas against Pathan and Afghan militants. BIA also provided troops to safeguard the assets of British in Aden, Iraq, Burma and Malaya. The first Global War, later known as World War I (WW I) began with the German Army attacking France via neutral Belgium.

Britain declared war against Germany. They combined forces with the French and opposed the advance of the German Army. They managed to halt the German Army advance in the plains of Flanders between Nieuport on the Belgian coast through the Artois, Ypres, Somme and Champagne up to the Swiss border. After the German advance was halted, both sides held this line entrenched with extensive defense works and obstacle systems. In effect this became the front line of the opposing Armies and was known as the Western Front. (There was an Eastern Front between Russia and Germany in the East). The British Expeditionary Forces held the Northern portion of the Western Front. The rest of the Western Front was held by the French.

In 1914, the British Forces suffered heavy causalities in July and August in their effort to prevent the German Army from reaching the Atlantic seacoast and attack France from the north and west. Britain could not find adequate manpower from the British Army to replace the casualties and reinforce the Western Front. Therefore, they decided to deploy BIA units in the Western Front along with British Army units. Accordingly Indian Expeditionary Force (IEF) 'A' comprising 1 and 2 Cavalry and 3 and 7 (Meerut) Indian Infantry Divisions were dispatched to Europe from India in September 1914. On their arrival they were deployed in the Ypres area in what was known as Ypres Salient in October 1914.

7 Infantry Division, henceforth referred as the Meerut Div, which consisted of Dehradun, Garhwal and Bareilly Brigades with seven BIA and five British Army Battalions had participated in the Second Battle of

Ypres in November 1914. 1/39 (Now 6 Mechanised Infantry Battalion) and 2/39 Garhwal Rifles (Now 2 Garhwal Rifles) were part of the Garhwal Brigade. 1/39 Garhwal was deployed against German Army near Festubert in France. The Unit prepared their defenses in adverse weather conditions. The new generation of magazine fed .303 Rifles issued to them recently had not been battle tested. In spite of these adverse circumstances, the Garhwalis readied themselves to fight against the German Army opposing them. The German Army opposing them were occupying trenches captured by them earlier in an attack against the British Army.

On 23 November 1914, 1/39 Garhwal Rifle was tasked to recapture the trenches lost to the Germans previously and to hold the captured objective. The attack involved crossing the no man's land, clearing obstacles, launching physical assault after throwing bombs (grenades) followed by close quarter fighting with bullets and bayonets. The Battalion planned to attack the objective from the flanks after artillery fire was lifted and the bombing parties have destroyed the trenches. The bayonet assault party would clear the bunkers in waves of assault troops followed by reserve troops.

On the night 23/ 24 November 1914, Capt Lumb was leading 1 Company from the left flank behind the bombing party. Naik Darwan Sigh was leading the assault of his section. While approaching the objective, he was wounded in his arm by the enemy fire. However he pressed on with the attack and captured the first trench. Once again he was wounded in the head and was bleeding profusely before he reached his final objective. With total disregard to his life he continued to lead his group and assaulted the enemy with fire and his bayonet and captured more trenches. By then he had lost a lot of blood and fell down unconscious. He was evacuated after the battle was over. The Company suffered 21 killed and 33 wounded.

The bravery exhibited by Naik Dharwan Singh Negi in the face of the enemy was recognized and he was awarded the Victoria Cross (VC) for gallantry. Capt Lumb and Subedar Dhan Singh of 1 Company were awarded Military Cross. King George V himself presented the VC to Naik Darwan Singh Negi on 05 December 1914. 1/39 Garhwal Rifles was awarded with the Battle Honour of Festubert.

In the First Battle of Ypres, 129 Baluch held defenses along the Western Front. The Germans launched a series of attack on 129 Baluch repeatedly.

Nk Darwan Singh Negi

Being Carried to the Hospital

The Baluchis fought back gallantly but they were overwhelmed by the numerically superior enemy. In the end, only Sepoy Khudadad Khan was left alive. He was seriously wounded, yet he continued firing his machine gun till the ammunition lasted. Though the attack was stalled, Khudadad Khan became unconscious and fell down. Later when he recovered, he managed to crawl back and reached his unit where he was given first aid and evacuated for treatment. For his extraordinary courage in the face of the enemy and devotion to duty, he was awarded the VC. (His unit is part of present Pakistan Army)

Later in the same Sector near Richebourg L'Avoue, 10 men of 15 Ludhiana Sikh under Lt John Smyth repeated the saga of the Battle of Saragarhi on 18 May 1915. Lt Smyth and 10 Sikh Sepoys were assigned a nearly impossible task of reinforcing and replenishing ammunition to one of their front line Company which was under attack. Two earlier attempts made by another unit did not succeed. Lt John Smyth (later major General) along with his 10 volunteers of 15 Ludhiana Sikh succeeded in delivering the bombs and ammunition bandoliers, but at a heavy cost. Lt Smyth reached the destination with just one more Sepoy left alive; Sepoy Lal Singh. He too was killed on reaching the destination. Thus all ten Sikhs died in the performance of their assigned task. Lt John Smyth was awarded with a VC. L/Nk Mangal Singh was decorated with IOM, the remaining were awarded with IDSM, all ten posthumously.

Thus the VC account was opened in the first battle in which Indians ever took part in Europe with three VCs in one battle. The Indian troops fighting in an alien environment with adverse climatic conditions against a strong German Army never lacked in bravery and self sacrifice. They were to win many more VCs and achieve greater glory for their country.

Darwan Singh Negi was born in 1883 at Karbatir village, near Karanprayag in the Chamoli, Garhwal (present day Uttarakhand). He was a Naik during the WW I. He was promoted to the rank of Jemadar in August 1915 and Subedar in October 1916. He retired and settled down in his village and died on 24 June 1950. One of his four sons joined the Indian Army and retired as Lt Col. The VC and other medals of Darwan Singh is in possession of his son.

GOBAR SINGH AT NEUVE CHAPELLE

After the Battle of Ypres in 1914, the British and German Forces strengthened their defenses along the Western Front and there was a near stalemate for over two months. By the beginning of 1915, a Division of the German Forces was withdrawn from the Western Front to strengthen the Eastern Front against Russia. This encouraged the Allies to launch an offensive against the Germans and force them to withdraw from the occupied areas in France. A victory was needed for the Allies to boost the morale of their Army which had suffered heavy casualties in the War until then. Neuve Chapelle was an important communication center the loss of which would affect Germans adversely. Therefore it was decided to launch an attack on Neuve Chapelle and capture it.

Neuve Chapelle

Neuve Chapelle was a French village 20 miles south of Ypres along the Western Front. The defenses around the village provided depth to an important logistic and communication center to the German Defenses during World War I. The German Army had two Divisions of their VII Corps holding the defenses in this sector at Neuve Chapelle which was based on the high ground at La Bassée. The railway line and the important town of Aubers were to its east in depth. Besides three British Divisions, the Indian Meerut and Lahore Divisions took part in the Battle of Neuve Chapelle in March 1915. This Battle witnessed many innovative methods of fighting which were adopted as standard practice in the future wars.

The plan was to break through the German Defenses at Neuve Chapelle with Infantry Divisions and fan out to the North and South. The Cavalry Division would then pass through the breach and encircle the Germans from the rear. In the subsequent phases, important high ground and railway facilities would be captured so as to prevent the Germans from using them for their logistic support. Heavy concentration of artillery barrage was planned before the attack to suppress the German fire and destroy the wire obstacles for the infantry to assault. Elaborate arrangements were also made to achieve surprise.

For the first time, maps based on the air photographs of the enemy defenses were made available to the attacking troops and artillery. Also, for the first time aircrafts were used to neutralise the enemy defenses and artillery for shifting barrages of fire just before the attack.

Along with British 8 Division, the Meerut Division was to assault across the obstacles and break through the defenses. Thereafter, Lahore Division with British 7 Division was to extend the breach on either side and capture more German defenses. The Meerut and Lahore Divisions which had participated in the Battle of Ypres in the North were part of the attacking Forces in the Battle of Neuve Chapelle.

The Meerut Division comprised Dehradun, Garhwal and Bareilly Brigades had both British and Indian Infantry battalions. 6 Jat, 1/9 GR, 1/39 Garhwal Rifle, 2/39 Garhwal Rifle, 2/3 GR, 41 Dogras and 2/8 GR were the Indian Infantry Battalions. Similarly the Lahore Division had Ferozpur, Jullender and Sirhind Brigades with 9 Bhopal, 15 Sikh, 47 Sikh, 1/1 GR and 1/ 4 GR Indian Infantry Battalions.

The Garhwal Brigade was tasked to capture a six hundred yards of the German bunker line on the south west of the Village. 2/39 Garhwal Rifles (Now 2 Garhwal Rifle) under the command of Lt Col Drake was the left assaulting battalion. The Battalion moved forward to the forming up place for assault before first light to avoid detection. 1 and 2 Company were to lead the assault.

The artillery bombardment commenced at 0730 hours on 10 March 1915 and the attack commenced at 0805 hours. 1 Company contacted the enemy and captured the front line trenches and in the second line they captured a machine gun and took some prisoners. Similarly the third line was crossed. When the assaulting party moved forward, they came under heavy automatic fire from behind an orchard. Several men were killed. They could not recommence their advance beyond that.

2 Company took more time after the artillery fire was shifted to reach the line of enemy trenches as they had to traverse longer distance. This gave the Germans adequate time to readjust their defenses. It appeared that the artillery fire was not effective in destroying the wire obstacles here. As a result, the opposition was much stronger. The German Defenses there were manned by the 12th Company of the 16th Regiment.

German Bunker

After crossing no man's land, 2 Company of Garhwal Rifle formed up in two lines. Then they crossed the obstacles where a passage through the wires was available and attacked the German bunkers. One of the leading sections was commanded by Nk Jaman Singh. They captured the first trench and forced the other Germans to withdraw by means of heavy bombing. Many Germans surrendered to Jaman Singh's Section. For this action Nk Jaman Singh was awarded the Indian Order of Merit.

The other half of the Company, having established a foothold, was expanding to their right. During the process of expansion, the leading party commander was killed. Rifleman Gobar Singh, who was a bayonet man with the bombers, took over the command and carried on attacking on the rest of the bunkers by bombing and bayoneting and took many prisoners. The Germans who escaped from there were caught in the fire of the neighboring British Battalion. While leading the attack on a machine gun detachment Gobar Singh was severely wounded. He continued his assault on the machine gun detachment and it was captured. After the capture of the machine gun, Sepoy Gobar Singh Negi collapsed and died of his wounds.

Garhwalis during the Attack

For his exceptional bravery and self sacrifice, Sepoy Gobar Singh Negi was awarded with Victoria Cross posthumously. Gobar Singh, son of Shri Badri Singh, was born on 7 October 1893 at Manjaur village near Chamba in Tehri Garhwal. He joined the Garhwal Rifles in October 1913.

Gobar Singh VC Memorial, Chamba

VC Memorial at Neuve Chapelle

In memory of Sepoy Gobar Singh Negi VC, an annual fair is organized by the Garhwal Rifle Regimental Center on 20/21 April in the area around the Negi Memorial in Chamba. During this fair, a large number of young Garhwalis are recruited into the Regiment which is very proud of heroes like Gobar Singh and Darwan Singh who were decorated with the highest bravery award of their time, the Victoria Cross.

RIDER GOBIND SINGH AT CAMBRAI

By the end of 1917, the Allies had stabilized the situation along the Western Front in WW I. Earlier in the Battle of Somme, both sides had suffered heavy casualties. It was apparent that the trench warfare was giving way to mobile battles. The horse cavalry was handicapped by the lack of means of communication to match their mobility. The casualties suffered in men and horses were enormous.

Cambrai was an important logistics center for the German Army in northern France. It was decided to break through the German Hindenburg Line of defensive positions and recapture this town before the winter set in. This would deny a major logistic base to the German Army. Between 20 November and 7 December 1917, a major battle was fought at Cambrai. This battle, known as the Battle of Cambrai, was different in many ways from the earlier battles.

Based on the recommendations made by his artillery commanders and JFC Fuller (later Major General; considered to be the originator of modern tank warfare tactics and a prominent military historian), a staff officer of the Royal Tank Corps, General Julian Byng, commander of the British Third Army decided to combine the infantry, artillery and the tanks as a single combat force to launch the attacks. The Battle of Cambrai is known for its first massed tank attack and the technique of preregistration of artillery targets before the attack.

Massed Tank Attack at Cambrai

Infantry following Tanks

The attack commenced at 0620 hours on 20 November 1917. Over 370 Mark IV tanks were employed for the massed attack. They were used to breach through the wire obstacles and provide protection to the infantry which followed the tanks. The artillery, besides providing quick fire support, undertook counter bombardment on the enemy artillery guns. They were able to fire barrages without registration (collection of firing data) of the target since the targets were already plotted on their map during the preparatory stage. This surprised the Germans completely. At the end of the day, the Allies had advanced two to three miles. This had never happened before.

During this Battle 5 Cavalry Brigade (Mhow) participated in the offensive as part of 2 Indian Cavalry Division. 2 Lancers was one of the Indian Regiment in the Brigade. On that day, 2 Lancers were tasked to capture a German Post. The Regiment advanced under heavy machine gun and artillery fire from a flank and captured their objective. They were ordered to exploit their success and gain more ground. 14 British Tanks which were to support them in the exploitation phase did not arrive. Therefore, the advance was resumed without waiting for the tanks. The horses either crossed through the gaps in the wire obstacles or jumped over it.

Lieutenant Broadway led one of the assaults. He had killed two Germans with his sword. He was about to kill another German officer, when the latter raised one of his hands as a sign of surrender. Broadway therefore spared his life. But the German officer, who held his pistol hidden behind him with his other hand, shot and killed Broadway. Even before Broadway fell, the treacherous German officer was killed with a lance by one of Broadway's men who was following him.

After the Post was captured, the Regiment came under machine gun fire and counter attack. By the morning of the next day, 2 Lancers was surrounded and cut off from the rest of the Brigade at the outskirts of village Epehy. The Brigade was at Peizieres which was about six miles away from the Regiment. The Regiment was out of communication with the Brigade Headquarter. The Commanding Officer wanted to send a rider with a message asking for help from the Brigade HQ. Two men volunteered. One was Lance Dafadar Gobind Singh and other was Sowar Jot Ram. Both were briefed to take separate route and each given a copy of the message.

Jot Ram took the shorter of the two routes. However he was killed by gunfire on his way. Gobind Singh took the longer route. The enemy spotted him and brought down machine gun fire on him. His horse was killed in the fire. Gobind Singh was wounded but did not stir pretending that he too was dead. The Germans did not fire at him again. After some time, he moved and dodging the Germans, Gobind Singh reached the Brigade HQs, having walked all the way, and delivered the message. He was given a new horse and asked to take back a message. Once again while riding back, he was shot at and his horse died. He had to walk more than half of his journey to reach his Regiment.

Gobind Singh

When the Commanding Officer wanted to send another message to the Brigade HQ, Gobind Singh once again volunteered and insisted that he is the only one who knew the route and the German disposition and hence was eminently qualified for the job. Though he was wounded, he was sent for the second time to the Brigade HQ. He was shot at and injured a third time and his horse cut into pieces. However, he reached the Brigade HQ and delivered the message. He requested that he be send back with the reply. But seeing his condition, he was denied permission. Subsequently troops were sent to reinforce 2 Lancers and the unit was saved from certain disaster.

For this act of dedication, exemplary courage and gallantry shown by Gobind Singh, he was awarded with the Victoria Cross.

Gobind Singh was born in village Damoi near Jodhpur in Rajasthan. He and his brother Amar Singh joined the Army in 1910. Both volunteered to serve with the IEF in Europe. However, on the advice of his Squadron Commander, Amar Singh was left behind in India to take care of his aged parents. On return from the War, Gobind Singh was given 100 acres of land. He retired as Jemadar and died in 1942 at his village Damoi.

CHATTA AND LALA ON THE BANKS OF TIGRIS

Mesopotamia (Iraq) literally means 'between two rivers' in Greek. The two major rivers, Tigris and Euphrates run from the north-west to the south-east of central Mesopotamia. They meet at Qurnah and from where it is known as Shatt Al Arab. Basrah is a major town located 40 miles south of Qurnah on the banks of the River. The River drains into Persian Gulf. The capital city is located on the banks of Tigris, 500 miles upstream from the Gulf. The land astride these rivers is flat and flood prone. Most towns existed on high grounds along the river banks.

Mesopotamia

Mesopotamia was a part of Turkish Ottoman Empire during World War I. Persia (Iran) was located to the east and Kuwait in the west of Mesopotamia and had good relation with Britain. The presence of large oil reserves in the northern and western parts of Mesopotamia was known by late 19th century. In the early years of 20th Century, Britain, France and Germany had secured long term contracts from the local rulers to explore, extract and export oil from Mesopotamia to their home land. The ships of British Navy were converted to run their engines with oil (from coal).

Hence it became strategically important to secure and maintain the oil fields of this region to keep their Navy afloat.

On the other hand, Germany developed close relationship with Turkey over a period of time. Ultimately Turkey became a member of the Central Power during WW I. The Turkish Army was trained with the help of German advisors and German Field Marshal Baron von der Goltz commanded the Ottoman Army in the crucial battles from 1914 to 1916.

Following the breakout of WW I in Europe, Turkey declared war against the Allied Forces. As a reaction to the declaration of War by Turkey, Britain decided to launch an offensive against the Turkish Army in Mesopotamia mainly with Indian Expeditionary Forces to secure the Britain's oil supply for the War.

During World War I, seven Indian Expeditionary Forces (IEF)'A to E,' were raised from the British Indian Army and sent to various theaters of War to fight along with the British Army. One of them was IEF D which was sent to Mesopotamia under General Barrett and later under Lt Gen Sir John Nixon. This Force, comprising one cavalry and seven infantry divisions, left Bombay on 16 October and reached the Persian Gulf on 23 October 1914. (Subsequently two more Indian Divisions from Europe joined this Force.) Poona Division was tasked to capture Basrah and protect the oil terminals and other important installations and transportation facilities located there.

This was achieved by 23 November and the oil refineries at Abadan were secured. The Ottoman's attempt to recapture Basrah was thwarted with heavy casualty on both sides. From there, Qurna (the river junction) was attacked and captured by 9 December by the British. 42 Ottoman officers and nearly 1,000 soldiers surrendered at Qurna. Further offensive along the river towards Bagdad was resumed in January 1915 with 6 Indian Division under Major General Townshend.

The advance progressed fast and Kut Al Amara (Kut) was captured by 7 October. The next objective, which turned out to be a tough nut to crack, was Ctesiphon which lies on the left bank of the Tigiris River. This town is located at 16 miles south of the capital Bagdad. The defense of Ctesiphon was conceived and prepared under German Marshal Baron von der Goltz.

After having advanced for 40 miles from Kut, the IEF met with a strong resistance from the Ottoman defense position at Ctesiphon on 22 November 1915. By the end of the day, the first line of trenches were captured but at a heavy cost. Due to heavy casualties and poor logistics support, the subsequent attacks did not succeed. On 24 November having reached a stalemate, Gen Townshend decided to stop further attack and fall back to Kut.

While the IEF was withdrawing to Kut, Baron von der Goltz directed his Army to follow them down the river. When Townshend halted at Kut, the Ottoman Army led a siege on Kut with large fresh forces. The Ottoman Army had established a good logistic chain to maintain the siege. Gen Townshend ordered his cavalry to break the siege and escape southwards which they did successfully. One month after the siege, Gen Townshend wanted to vacate the remaining army from Kut. This was not agreed to by Gen Nixon.

A large-sized force was assembled by the Allied Forces at Ali Gharbi under General Aylmer, commander of the Tigris Corps, to break the siege of the Ottoman Army at Kut. By then, besides the three Divisions which were part of Tigris Corps, the Lahore and Meerut Division from Western Front in Europe had also joined the IEF D. On 6 January 1916, the Tigiris Corps advanced along both banks of Tigiris towards Sheik Saad on the way to Kut.

Here the defenses were well concealed and hence the exact disposition of Ottoman forces could not be assessed. Later the defenses were contacted with the help of locals and fierce battle followed. Some success was achieved on the Right Bank of the River on the first day. Finally on 9 January 1916 the Ottomans withdrew from Sheikh Saad. Over the following two days no tangible result could be achieved due to heavy rains.

The Ottomans retreated from Sheikh Saad to Wadi. Wadi in Arabic means valley. It was a steep valley of a stream that ran from the north into the River Tigris 6 miles from Sheikh Saad towards Kut. The defenses were on the steep embankment. Wadi had to be cleared before the siege at Kut could be broken.

The Tigris Corps under Gen Aylmer attacked the Left bank of the Wadi Defenses on 13 January 1916. 7 Meerut Division and 3 Lahore Division which had joined the Force from Europe participated in this attack. During the attack the Commanding officer (CO) of 9 Bhopal Infantry battalion was seriously wounded and was lying in the open.

Sepoy Chatta Singh who was engaging the enemy from behind a cover realized that his CO was wounded and lying in the open. With total disregard to his safety, he moved out of his cover and reached the spot where the CO was lying. He dressed the wound of his CO and immediately made a sand wall around his CO to protect him from enemy fire. The CO could not be evacuated immediately due to intense enemy fire. Later he lay down near his wounded CO to provide protection from enemy fire. After sunset the CO was evacuated.

Sepoy Chatta Singh Protecting his Wounded CO (Painting)

For this act of exemplary courage and loyalty beyond the call of duty exhibited under enemy fire, Sepoy Chatta Singh was awarded the Victoria Cross, the highest award for bravery during war. It was presented to him in the field on 8 March 1916.

Chatta Singh was born at Tilsada Village in Kanpur in 1886. He joined 9 Bhopal Infantry and participated in the Battles of Ypres and Neuve Chapelle in the Western Front in Europe before his unit came to Mesopotamia where he was awarded VC. He retired as Havaldar and lived in his village until he died on 23 March 1961.

Hav Chatta Singh VC with General Rajendra Sinji (COAS) in 1953

During the night of 13/14 January 1916, preparations were underway to launch further attack on Wadi Defenses on the following day. The next day it was found that the Turks had vacated from the Wadi Defenses, hence no attack was launched on that day. The Tigris Corps in their effort to break the siege of Kut advanced further and met with a strong resistance at Hanna between the Tigris River and Suwaikiya Marsh on the Right Bank of the River.

Attack against Hanna defenses was launched on 21 January on a broad frontage of 1200 yards. 37 Dogras (now 7 Mech Inf) and 41 Dogras (now 3 Dogra) which were part of 21 and 35 Brigades respectively attacked ferociously. The defenders opened up with large number of machine gun fire. The attacking troops suffered very heavy casualties. The CO of 37 Dogra, Lt Col McCrea and Capt Nicholson were injured seriously and Lt Fayer was killed during the attack. The CO of 37 Dogra was evacuated and saved by Jemadar Tara Chand of 41 Dogra. Unfortunately, Tara Chand was fatally injured later while evacuating other wounded men. He was awarded with the Indian Order of Merit posthumously.

Capt Nicholson was lying wounded when L/NK Lala Ram of 41 Dogra saw him and rushed towards him under fire. After dressing his wounds, Lala shifted him into a shallow trench to protect him from enemy fire. While attending Capt Nicholson, Lala heard the voice of Lt Lindop asking for help. Lala rushed to the spot under enemy fire where Lindop was lying injured. After bandaging his wounds he wanted to shift him to safety. Lt Lindop did not permit him to be carried as it would have certainly endangered both of them from enemy fire during day light hours. Lala stayed with Lindop until evening when he went to his trenches and came back with stretcher bearers and evacuated Lindop for treatment. For the conspicuous gallantry and unflinching loyalty, L/Nk Lala Ram was awarded VC on 21 January 1915.

Jemadar Lala Ram VC

Lala Ram was born on 20 April 1876 at Parol village in District Kangra, Punjab. He joined the Dogras on 20 February 1901. He participated in the Battles of Wadi and Hanna. Later he was promoted to the rank of Jemadar and retired from the Army after serving for over 20 years. He died in his village on 23 March 1927.

The Tigiris Corps made many attempts to break the siege at Kut, but did not succeed. On 29 April the garrison of Kut with 13,000 men of Tigris Corps surrendered to Ottoman Forces. This was one of the major tragedies for the Allies in WW I. Most prisoners died of hunger and ill treatment.

The Tigiris Corps resolved to capture Kut. Extensive preparations were made before the offensive operations were resumed. Administrative support was improved and the fighting potential of Tigris Corps was enhanced. The Corps resumed the advance along both Banks of the River and captured Kut on 16 December.

By March 17, Bagdad was captured and the people of Bagdad were assured that the British had come to liberate them and not to rule over them. The Ottomans in Mesopotamia were finally defeated and evicted from there in the Battle of Sharqat on 23 October 1918 in which a large number of BIA Units had participated. Shortly after that, WW I ended on the 31 Of October 1918.

DEBACLE AT DARDANELLES

The Allies realized that fighting war along the Western Front in Europe during World War I (WW I) was going to be a long and costly one. They were in search of an alternative strategy to defeat the Central Power. Besides the stalemate in the Western Front, the Russians perceived a viable threat developing from Turkey. In order to tie down the Turks and Germans, Britain decided to open Multiple Fronts in the East.

One such adventure was a naval assault through Dardanelles followed by an attempt to capture Constantinople and link up with Russians. This would also break the blockade imposed for the Allies Shipping through the Dardanelles by the Central Power on 29 October 1914. The Dardanelles, also known as Hellespont, is a 38 miles long, three quarter mile to four miles wide and 180 feet deep strait in Turkey connecting the Aegean Sea to the Sea of Marmara. About this strait it is said that the water flows in both direction; surface current and under current flow in the opposite direction simultaneously.

The British Naval attack began on 19 February 1915. It was a disaster from the beginning of the operation. The weather was bad and demining operations were impeded by the heavy and accurate fire by the Turks artillery guns from the coast. Three battle ships were sunk and the narrow strait was chocked up presenting attractive targets to the Turks bombardment.

A second attack was launched on 25 February by the British Navy. This time it succeeded partially and the Turks withdrew to the next defense line. However no further advance could be launched due to strong interference from the Turks holding the Gallipoli Peninsula. Therefore it was decided to attack and capture the Gallipoli Peninsula by land operations before the naval operations could be resumed towards Constantinople.

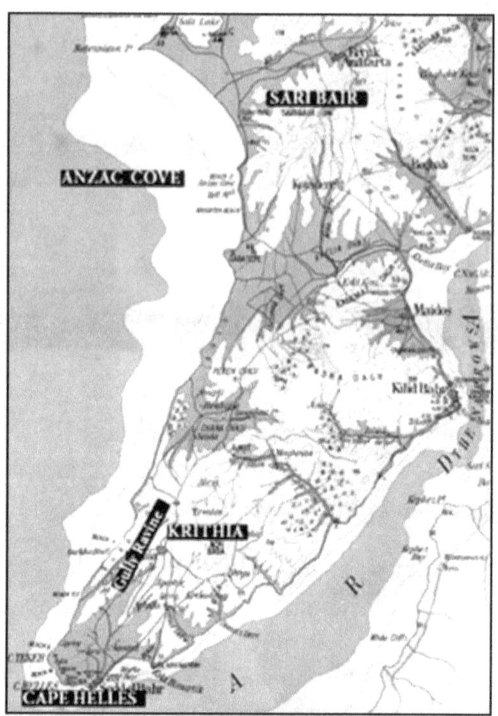

Gallipoli Peninsula

Initially Britain assembled five divisions known as Mediterranean Expeditionary Force comprising British, French, Australian, New Zealand and Indian Army. 29 Indian Brigade comprising 14 Sikh (Ferozpur), 1/6 Gurkha Rifles and 2/10 Gurkha Rifles was sent from Egypt to be attached with British 29 Division. By the time the troops arrived and landed at Cape Helles at the southern tip and at Anzac Cove in the west of the peninsula, the Turks had enough reaction time to prepare their defenses thoroughly. They had six divisions defending the Peninsula under Mustafa Kemel Pasa and Lt Gen Otto Sanders, a German Army General.

The Allies landing commenced on 25 April 1915. The plan was to advance with the 29 Division from the Southern tip towards North and for the Australian and New Zealand (ANZAC) Division to advance from Cove in the west in order to trap and destroy the retreating Turk Army. The landing in the South was contested by the defenders.

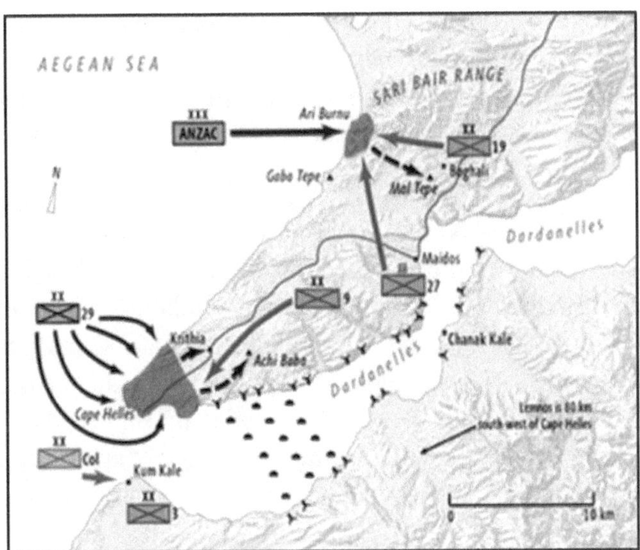

The Attack Plan

However 29 Division managed to establish initial foothold on the Beach at Helles although with heavy casualties. In addition to the British 29 Division, the French Forces joined in the offensive towards the Village Krithia in the North. The attack on Krithia was launched on 28 April. The attack did not succeed. The stalemate lasted till 6 May when the second attack was launched on Krithia. The attackers suffered heavily and advanced only half a mile.

The final attack on Krithia was launched on 4 June in which 14 (Ferozpur) Sikh was tasked to capture two enemy trench lines known as J10 and J11 astride Galley Ravine. Those defenses were well coordinated with obstacles and covered with machine gun fire. The attack commenced on broad daylight at 1100 hours after a brief artillery fire. The artillery fire was not effective against the trenches with strong overhead protection. The Sikhs fought ferociously against the Turks under murderous machine gun fire from the enemy trenches. When the wire obstacles remained intact, the Sikhs jumped over the barbed wire and engaged the Turks in close quarter battle with bayonets. However the fire power from the defenses overwhelmed the brave attackers.

General Sir Ian Hamilton the Commander of the Expeditionary Force G was impressed by the bravery of the Sikhs and had paid rich tribute to the heroism of all ranks of the 14 Sikhs. Out of 15 officers only three were not wounded. Although the Sikhs captured a part of their objective, it was at a heavy cost. The Battalion was nearly wiped out. They lost more than 370 officers and men on that day. In this operation, the Gurkhas attacking from the left captured a near vertical cliff which was later named as Gurkha Bluff.

In the west the ANZAC landing was successful after the initial setback. They captured the beaches and established a beachhead south of Sari Bari Ranges. While they were consolidating and attempting to expand the initial foothold, the Turks under Mustafa Kemal attacked the beachhead. But the ANZAC held on to their defenses and beaten back the attack with the help of naval gunfire. Once again on 19 May, the Turks launched another massive counter attack. It did not succeed. The Turks suffered more than 10,000 dead and wounded in their counter attacks against the ANZAC.

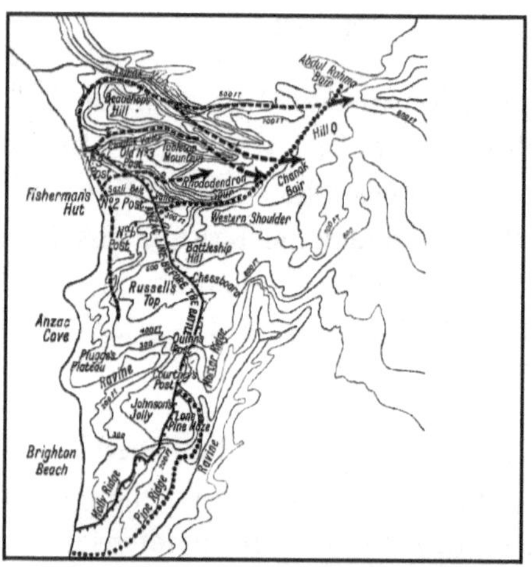

The Attack Plan on Sari Bair

In the month of August, General Hamilton made a final attempt to turn the Turks Front by attempting to capture the dominating heights of Sari Bair Ranges which overlooks a vast region in the North. He launched two divisions to the North of ANZAC Cove; with diversionary attacks at Helles and ANZAC Cove. Perceiving the threat developing from North, the Turks quickly occupied the defenses at the higher hills overlooking the areas south wound west of Sari Bair. In this operation 29 Indian Brigade was tasked to capture Hill 971 and Battl Q. Chunuk Bair to the south of Hill Q was the objective of the New Zealand Brigade in which 2/10 GR also participated in the offensive.

Attack commenced with artillery bombardment on 6 August. 1/6 GR which was part of 29 Brigade moved through difficult and unfamiliar terrain. By 1800 hours on 8 August, they reached 200 feet from their objective at Q Hill. Most of the other battalions either had lost their way or were pinned down by the Turks Army opposition. In their final assault, the Gurkhas assaulted their objective and after a severe bayonet and hand-to-hand fight with Turks, they captured it on the morning of August 9. It looked as if the Turks had been defeated at Sari Bair and Gallipoli at last could be captured.

One of the young officers of a neighboring Royal Warwickshire Battalion watched the Gurkhas fighting the Turks with awe and admiration. He decided to join the brave Gurkhas and later applied for a transfer. This materialized after the War. Later this young officer became a Field Marshal and commanded the Fourteenth Army in WW II. He was Field Marshal Viscount William 'Bill' Slim of whom more is written in this book.

Although the Gurkhas suffered heavy casualties, were tired and there was no reserves available, Major Allanson who led the Battalion to victory at Q Hills decided to pursue the withdrawing Turks. After about 200 yards of advance, the Gurkhas came under artillery barrage that included the Q Hill. Going back and reorganizing on their objective would have been disastrous.

Without any reinforcement, the Gurkhas were forced to withdraw from their captured objective. No other unit had reached anywhere close to their objective against the devastating machine gun fire of the Turks. The operation was called off on the 9th of August.

Another attempt was made on 21 August by the Allies to capture the Peninsula; this time from Sulva Bay. Fighting in the extreme climatic condition was a bad idea. The attack on Hill 60 and Scimitar Hill was beaten back with heavy casualties. By 29 August the offensive ended in a failure and the future of Gallipoli Campaign looked to have reached its conclusion. By the end of November, orders were issued to the Expeditionary Force G to evacuate Gallipoli. The last of the troops left Gallipoli on 10 January 1916.

Thus ended the Campaign launched to capture Gallipoli Peninsula in a Debacle. Approximate casualties both dead and wounded of the Allies were estimated to be about 140 thousand. On the other hand the Turks were known to have suffered about 190 thousand casualties. Nearly 50% of the Allies soldiers suffered from fever and diarrhea.

Although the Turks were defeated in the end of WW I, the successful defense of Gallipoli was a defining moment for the Turks and the Central Power. It was a disaster for the Allies. They could not open the second front that they so badly needed.

BRAVE BADLU SINGH IN PALESTINE

The Central Power (Axis) during World War I (WW I) consisted of Germany, the Austro-Hungarian Empire, Bulgaria and the Ottoman Empire. Present day Iraq, Turkey, Syria, Palestine, Israel, Lebanon, Jordon, Saudi Arabia and part of Egypt were under Ottoman Empire. The war in the Western Front between the Allies and Central Power had reached a stalemate and was proving expensive to both sides to continue.

Britain was not able to replace casualties with British troops fast enough to continue the War relentlessly. With the vast resources available to them from their colonies in the east, the Allies planned to open multiple fronts away from the Western Front to defeat the Central Power. Accordingly, the Allies with the help of their colonial forces from India and Australia opened additional fronts against the Central Power in the Dardanelles, Iraq and Palestine.

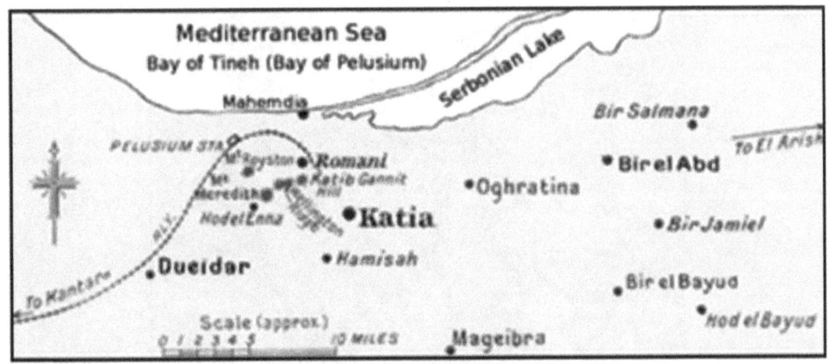

Romani and Katia

Gallipoli Front was opened to advance into Black Sea and link up with Russian eastern Front in February 1915. War in Iraq came to a grinding halt with the debacle at Kut. Under these circumstances the third possible Front in Sinai and Palestine emerged slowly. The Suez Canal was defended by holding the dominating areas east of the Canal between Port

Said and Port Suez by the Commonwealth Army. Bulk of this Army came from the Indian Army comprising Sikhs, Baluchis, Gorkhas and Bikaner Camel Corps. The northern defense node was based in and around Katia extended up to Romani in the north. Katia was about 18 miles east of Suez Canal.

On 26 January 1915, the Ottoman Army with German assistance made an attempt to capture the Suez Canal. Their raid on the Canal was frustrated by the alert Allies protective elements. Once again the Axis Forces attacked Katia with strong contingents. They succeeded in capturing Katia on 23 April. The third attack came on Romani on 3 August 1916. This time the Allies were better prepared and defeated the combined Ottoman Forces by 12 August 1916. With that the Ottoman threat to Suez Canal ended. The Allies were poised to enter Palestine.

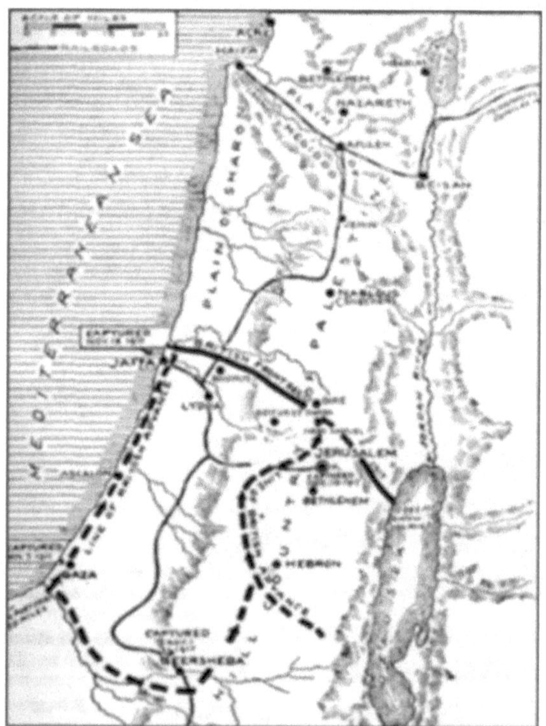

Palestine

Palestine is situated between the Mediterranean Sea in the west and the Jordon River in the east. This narrow strip of land had seen many kingdoms and rulers from the ancient times. Finally it came under Ottoman

Empire in the early years of sixteenth century. Palestine was held by the Ottoman with her allies in the Central Power; the German and Austrian Army in the beginning of WW I.

Having succeeded in the Battle of Romani, Britain ordered an offensive into Sinai with the view to destroy the Ottoman Forces deployed there and capture Palestine. Allies Egyptian Expeditionary Forces (EEF) made an attempt to capture Gaza in March 1917. It did not succeed. Another attempt was made in April which also ended in failure.

At that stage of the War, one of the most successful Generals of WW I, General Sir Edmund Allenby was appointed as the overall commander of the EEF in Palestine with a mandate to capture Jerusalem by December 1917. Indian 4 and 5 Cavalry Divisions, 3 Lahore Division, 7 Meerut Division, Jodhpur, Hyderabad and Mysore Lancers and Bikaner Camel Corps were part of the General Allenby's Army in Palestine.

On taking over the Command on 27 June 1917, having assessed the ground situation, General Allenby asked for additional resources for the planned Palestine offensive operations and he got them all. He decided to tackle Beersheba first. He undertook many deception measures while launching the attack on Beersheba. The Ottomans were expecting the next attack on Gaza. They were completely surprised when Beersheba was attacked. It was one of the most successful cavalry charges made in WW I; probably the last one on 31 October 1917.

The Battle of Beersheba ended in a complete victory for the British on 6 November. The Ottoman Forces had conducted an orderly withdrawal delaying the British Forces which was advancing towards Northern Palestine. The next day (7 November), Gaza was attacked for the third time and was captured.

While withdrawing, after vacating a few delaying lines, the Ottomans Army had established a defense line joining Bethlehem to Jerusalem and on to Jaffa. Between 17 November and 9 December 1917, the battle for Jerusalem was fought. In the end, on 9 December, Jerusalem was captured. At last, the Allies had achieved their first major victory after three long years of war. Later, on 22 December, Jaffa was also captured. This was the turning point in the operations against the Central Power in Palestine. General Allenby ordered his Army to pursue the withdrawing Ottoman Army which was assisted by the German Army Officers.

Allenby's Army followed on the heels of retreating Ottoman Army to the North. Their attempt to delay the advancing forces was thwarted by fast moving cavalry operations. Finally the Ottoman Army in Palestine gave one last battle in the Hills of Judea. General Liman von Sanders was the new Commander of the German Asia Corps. The operations in the Jordan Valley and Judea Hills were fought at the strategically important towns of Haifa, Sharon and Nablus.

Allenby Walking into Jerusalem

In the Battle of Haifa a squadron of Mysore Lancers and Jodhpur Lancers effectively defeated the German rear guards and captured Haifa. The bravery and tenacity of Indian Cavalry men in this battle ultimately contributed to the fall of Ottoman Forces in Palestine. Major Dalpat Singh, who died of his wound suffered during the daring assault on the Turks, Capt Anop Singh and 2/Lt Sagat Singh were awarded the Military Cross for bravery. Capt Aman Singh and Dafadar Jor Singh were awarded the Indian Order of Merit.

2 Lancers were moved from the Western Front from France for Egypt in February 1918 to join Allenby's advancing Army during the occupation of Jordan Valley. During the Battle of Megiddo, the Regiment under Lt Col Davison launched a daring quick attack in the Jezreel Valley and broke the Ottoman defenses there. This paved the way subsequently to destroy the Ottoman Forces from this valley. For his daring act of bravery, Davison was awarded DSO.

Indian Lancers Riding into Haifa

14th Murray's Jat Lancers was attached to 29 Lancers (Deccan Horse) in Palestine. After the capture of Nebulas, Allenby's Army advanced northwards into Judea Hills. 29 Lancers were part of the advancing Army. The Regiment was tasked to advance and round up the retreating Ottoman forces on the west bank between the Jordan River and the village Khan-e-Samariyeh on 23 September 1918. While advancing, the Regiment was opposed by the enemy from the strongly-held Twin Hill feature. 14th Murray's Jats were tasked to clear the opposition. A Squadron attack was launched with Risaldar Badlu Singh leading his troops from the left-side.

While approaching the objective, the Squadron was fired upon from an unexpected enemy position from a dominating hill on the left of the objective with machine guns and rifles and caused casualty. Having realized the importance of clearing the interfering locality, Risaldar Badlu Singh collected a small detachment of six Jat Lancers under his command and with utter disregard to his safety charged the enemy in a lightening dash.

The enemy was shocked but had put up a stiff fight. During the assault Badlu Singh was wounded while fighting against a machine gunner single handedly on top of the hill. In spite of his wound, he continued to fight and captured the objective and took the surrender of the enemy. After the task was completed, he collapsed on the objective and died of excessive bleeding from his wounds.

Risaldar Badlu Singh

His action saved heavy casualty to the attacking troops. This in turn resulted in the capture of the objective. For this act of supreme courage, valor and initiative of the highest order and self sacrifice, Risaldar Badlu Singh was awarded Victoria Cross posthumously.

Badlu Singh was born in village Dhakla near Jhajjar in present day Haryana in November 1876. He rose to the rank of Risaldar when his unit arrived in Palestine. His VC Medal is displayed at Lord Ashcroft Gallery in the Imperial War Museum, London. His name is engraved in the Heliopolis War Cemetery in Cairo.

The Palestine Campaign ended along with the WW I on 11 November 1918. The Allies emerged victorious with the surrender of Ottomans at Damascus earlier. Throughout the Palestine Campaign, the Indian Infantry and Cavalry units played a significant role in the capture of Palestine. Many memorials have been erected in the present day Israel commemorating the bravery and sacrifices made by the Indians in evicting the Ottomans from Palestine.

ISHAR IN THE LAND OF PASHTUNWALI

Pashtunwali is an unwritten code of conduct which the Pastuns who inhabited on both sides of the border of Afghanistan and British India known as Waziristan followed for many centuries. Honour, bravery, loyalty, hospitality and revenge are some of the important principles of Pashtunwali. Wazirs and Mehsuds are two major tribes in Waziristan.

Numerous attempts were made by the British since 1850 to encroach into Waziristan and rule over the Pashtuns unsuccessfully. Waziristan was part of North West Frontier Province (NWFP) created by Lord Curzon in 1901. The NWFP comprised five districts and the Tribal Administered Frontier Fgencies including North and South Waziristan.

British India Boundary

On 8 August 1919 the Anglo Afghan Treaty was signed after the Third Afghan War. According to this treaty British India agreed that their troops will not cross the Khyber Pass into Afghanistan and recognized Afghanistan as an independent country. Durant Line was accepted as the boundary between the two countries by both parties. Thereafter the British stopped all the subsidies to Afghanistan.

The British had earlier raised Militia units to maintain law and order in Waziristan on both sides of Durant Line. After the Anglo Afghan Treaty, those Militia men on the western side of the Border abandoned their posts and deserted along with their weapons. They came to the eastern side of the Durant Line and joined their fellow tribesmen to fight against the British influence in Waziristan.

After having formalised the border with Afghanistan, the British attempted to gradually assimilate Waziristan with the rest of India by developing the area. They established posts all along the border and got down to improving the lines of communication in Waziristan. Wana in the South-west was made into a major military post. While the trans-border situation had somewhat stabilized, the internal insurgency problem persisted.

The freedom loving Pashtuns, Mehasuds and Wazirs were against any rule of law other than their own tribal rules. The deserters from the Militia with their weapons along with the locals attacked the British Army units whenever they ventured out of their camps. To control insurgency, the British Indian Army units known as Waziristan Field Forces were stationed in the major communication centers and towns. It was planned to create a brigade-size cantonment in Waziristan at Razmak with large number of outposts spread throughout Waziristan.

Besides road construction the Army units were involved in establishing posts and providing protection to the convoys. 28 Punjab was operating in the area of Wana. The fierce Mahsuds in this area were constantly harassing the British Forces by their hit and run operations. Therefore, all movements were conducted tactically with proper protection.

28 Punjab was tasked to establish military post to dominate the area. On 10 April 1921, 28 Punjab was advancing along Haidari-Shakan Road in South Waziristan providing protection to a convoy. On that day there was a strong dust storm and visibility was poor. They passed through a defile between two hills at Haidari Kach. When the advance guard of the battalion was moving between the two hills, they came under heavy fire.

Sepoy Ishar Singh was with the Lewis Gun detachment as the Number 1 gunner. He identified the location from where the enemy fire was coming and directed heavy automatic fire on the enemy killing many. Nearly a hundred Mahsuds were firing at the advancing column. An attack

Sepoy Ishar Singh with Lewis Gun

was launched and hand-to-hand fight ensued. Ishar Singh was injured in the chest and his gun was snatched by the enemy.

Though wounded, Ishar gathered two more men and charged the enemy and took back his gun from the enemy. He brought the gun into action and killed many of the fleeing enemy. In this attack his company officers and a few NCOs were killed. By now, Ishar was bleeding. His commander told him to go to a safer place and get his wound dressed.

While going to get his wound dressed, Ishar saw many of his comrades lying wounded. The Mahsuds were still firing. He decided to help those who were more severely wounded and save their life by providing first aid, evacuating them for treatment and providing them with drinking water. He also provided protection to the medical officer and assisted him in treating the other wounded. After about two hours, he became weak due to bleeding and decided to get his wound dressed.

By his brave action and compassion he inspired many. On that day more than 50 men were killed or injured. The Mahsuds suffered more casualties. After the delay due to the attack, the Battalion resumed the advance. Sepoy Ishar Singh was awarded Victoria Cross for his most conspicuous bravery and devotion to his duty. The Medal was awarded to him by the Prince of Wales in March 1922 at Rawalpindi.

The Prince of Wales decorating the First Sikh VC

Ishar was invited for VC dinner in 1929 and attended many ceremonial functions. He participated in WW II as Subedar and was awarded with Order of British India and promoted to the rank of Captain. He was given 75 Acres of land and provided with a house.

Captain Ishar Singh VC, OBI

Ishar Singh was born at Nenwan in Punjab on 30 December 1895. He died on 2 December 1963.

PERSEVERING BHAGAT

After the Berlin Conference was held in 1884 during which the method of colonization in Africa was formalized by the European nations, most African states were colonized for political, economic and social advantages. Britain, Italy and Germans had their colonies in East Africa. The Horn of Africa comprises Eritrea, Djibouti, Ethiopia and Somalia located on the west coast of Red Sea. Sudan is situated to the west of Eritrea and Ethiopia. Eritrea is in the North of Ethiopia. North and East of Eritrea are covered by the Red Sea. Across the Red Sea to the East is Saudi Arabia and Yemen. Italy had colonized Eritrea, Ethiopia and Somalia by 1936. As against this, Britain had occupied Egypt for the defense of Suez Canal including Sudan.

Until June 1940, Italy - being the weaker member of the Axis Power - did not join WW II. In June 40, Italy somehow perceived that the War in Europe was going to end in favor of Germany soon. Therefore, Italy decided to join the War to benefit from the spoils of WW II. They declared war against the Allies on 10 June primarily to expand her colonial territory in Africa.

Mussolini decided to attack and capture the British and French colonies. Accordingly, on 04 July 1940, the Italian Forces crossed their border from Eritrea to the West and captured the border towns of Kassala and Gallabat in Sudan. Due to logistic constraints, the Italian Forces were not able to advance further; they consolidated their initial gains and held Kasssala with a brigade size force.

Britain decided to launch a counter offensive to recapture Kassala and Gallabat and the entire Eretria including Asmara, the Capital City and Massama the Port City. General Archibald Wavell who evicted the Ottomans from Palestine successfully during the WW I was appointed as the Commander-in-Chief of the Common Wealth Forces assembled for the offensive in East Africa. 4 and 5 Indian Divisions along with large number of British Indian Army Units were part of this Force.

10 Brigade of 5 Indian Division, commanded by Brigadier Bill Slim MC (later Field Marshal), was tasked to attack and recapture Gallabat and capture Metamma which is inside Eritrea. Adequate air support, artillery, tanks and 21 Field Company, Royal Bombay Sappers and Miners were allotted to 10 Brigade for this task. 21 Field Company Bombay Engineers was commanded by the young Second Lieutenant Premindra Singh Bhagat.

10 Brigade launched the attack on Gallabat on 6 November 1940. 3/18 Garhwal Rifle was on the lead. The attack commenced at 0510 hours and Gallabat was captured by 0800 hours. Further advance to Metamma could not be undertaken due to non-availability of tanks which were to lead the attack and destroy the wire obstacles in front of Italian strong defense works at Metamma. Their repair and recovery delayed the attack. This gave enough time to Italians to counter attack 10 Brigade at Gallabat.

The Italian Air Forces bombed Gallabat and followed it by ground attack that caused heavy casualty for the troops of 10 Brigade. 10 Brigade could not hold on to their recaptured positions against the Italian counter attack. They were ordered to withdraw from Gallabat to a Ridge three miles west of Gallabat. During the withdrawal, 21 Field Company Engineers was tasked to obstruct and delay the pursuing Italian Forces to avoid any interference to the withdrawing troops of 10 Brigade.

As part of his plan to delay the Italians, 2/Lt Bhagat decided to demolish a culvert with large quantity of explosives filled in two broken down tanks and placed over the culvert. When the enemy closed in with the culvert, the tanks filled with charges were detonated. While one of the tanks exploded, the other did not.

Knowing the importance of destroying the Culvert, Bhagat rushed to the second explosive filled tank and re-primed the demolition charges and detonated the second tank which resulted in the destruction of the culvert and delayed the enemy advance. All this while, he was under enemy fire. For this act of bravery, he was recommended for a Military Cross. Later his name was mentioned in the Dispatches for bravery.

10 Brigade was relieved by 9 Brigade from Gallabat in November 1940. By January 1941, the British had decided to commence their offensive into Eritrea. General Wavell undertook many deception measures to conceal the intended thrust line to Asmara. 9 Brigade was tasked to capture Metemma in the South. In the North, the British advanced towards Keren. By 31 January after having lost Agordat, the Italians realized that the main offensive was directed towards Keren in the north. Therefore they vacated Metemma and withdrew towards Gondar.

9 Brigade had quickly occupied Metemma. 3/12 Royal Frontier Force (Later Sikh LI) under Lt Col Blood was tasked to pursue the withdrawing Italian Forces. Along with him was 2/Lt PS Bhagat with a detachment of engineers to provide engineer support to the Mission. It involved creating passage through a number of deep enemy minefields. Bhagat was moving with his detachment in the leading Bren Carrier; a light tracked vehicle with armor protection and machine gun mounted.

While crossing an unsuspected minefield, his carrier went over a mine and was blown off. The Carrier was damaged beyond repair. However the occupants of the Bren Carrier escaped unhurt. Bhagat shifted into another Bren carrier. Once again his carrier was blown off in a minefield. The driver and the sapper who was travelling with him were killed.

Bhagat got down from the carrier and whereever he suspected a possible minefield on his way, he physically searched the area for mines and defused it when came across a mine lying in the path of the carrier. Although this slowed down the move, this procedure saved many lives. They continued their advance for three days.

On the fourth day his carrier went over a mine and was damaged. This time, Bhagat was injured. His ear drum was punctured and bleeding.

In spite of his injury, he refused to be evacuated and insisted on being part of his mission. When he was asked to go for treatment, he argued that he was the best person suited for the job as he had gained a lot of experience defusing fifteen mines during the past four days. There was no one else to replace him. Finally after completing the mission, he was relieved as he was utterly exhausted and bleeding from his ear. He was evacuated to Khartoum where he was treated for his injury.

For his longest recorded feat of sheer cold courage, 2/Lt Premindra Singh Bhagat was awarded with the Victoria Cross. In June 41, General Wavell presented the VC Ribbon at Asmara during the Victory parade. Later, Lord Linlithgow, the then Viceroy of India honored 2/LT Bhagat with the VC Medal at New Delhi on 10 November 1941.

Lt PS Bhagat VC

Premindra Singh Bhagat was born on 13 October 1918 at Gorakhpur UP. His father Surendra Singh Bhagat was an engineer. He joined Royal Indian Military College in 1930 and Indian Military Academy in 1937. On 15 July 1939 he was commissioned into the Royal Bombay Sappers and Miners. His first posting was to 21 Field Company of Royal Bombay Sappers.

Second Lieutenant Premindra Singh Bhagat was the first and the only Indian Officer to be awarded with the VC; the highest gallantry award by the British. After Independence he rose to the rank of Lt Gen and became the Central Army Commander. His two elder brothers were also in the Army; eldest in Engineers who passed out with the First Course from the IMA and another in the Corps of Signals.

SUBEDAR RICHPAL AT KEREN

Italy entered the Second World War against Allies on 10 June 1940. She decided to expand her North and East African colonies by capturing the neighboring French and British colonies. As part of the overall plan, Italy launched her forces from Eritrea and Ethiopia into Sudan and captured the border towns of Kassala and Gallabat on 4 July 1940. General Archibald Wavell, the overall commander of British Commonwealth Forces was directed to plan an offensive into Italian colony of Eritrea and Ethiopia with a view to capture those Italian colonies and evict the Italian Forces from East Africa to ensure a safe passage through Red Sea and Suez Canal to the Commonwealth Forces.

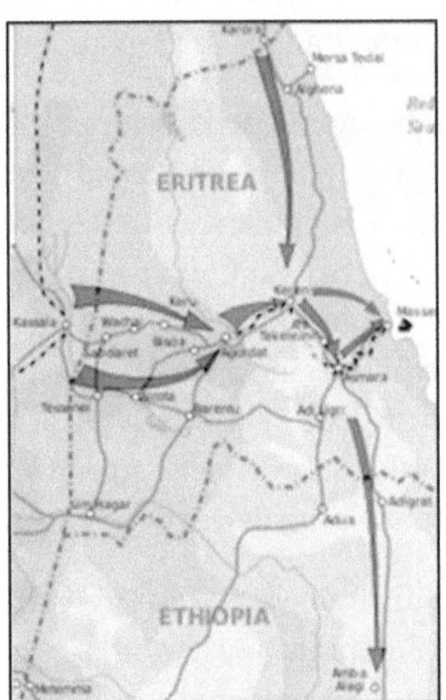

Offensive Plan - Eritrea

One of the thrust lines planned was from Sudan, through Eritrea and into Ethiopia from the North. This involved the capturing of major towns/ cities and communication centers of Kassala, Agordat, Keren, Massama and Asmara. Lt Gen William Platt was given the command of Indian 4 and 5 Divisions along with adequate resources for this task. Later more forces including air efforts were allotted at the critical stages as the battles progressed. The counter offensive was planned to be launched on 08 Febraury1941.

The Italian Overall Force Commander in Eritrea was the Duke of Aosta. The Italian offensive plan to capture Sudan was aborted after the capture of the border towns of Kassala and Gallabat due to lack of fuel for tanks and local support. Having appreciated the possibility of a counter offensive by the British Commonwealth Forces into Eritrea and Ethiopia by early 1941, the Duke redeployed the Italian Forces to defend the strategically important cities by holding them strongly at Agordat, Keren, Asmara and Massama.

To meet the troop requirement for the redeployment of the forces, Kassala which was far away from the capital, was vacated by the Italian Army on 17 January 41. Having deduced the likely pattern of Italian Defense Plan, General Platt decided to launch the offensive earlier on 19 January instead of the originally scheduled 08 February 41 which would have given more time to the Italians to prepare their new defenses.

4 and 5 Divisions comprised British Indian Army and other Commonwealth Army Units. 4 Division had 5, 7 and 11 Brigades with 1, 14 and 16 Punjab, 1 and 4 Rajputana Rifles, 11 Sikh, 4th Battalion of 7 Rajput and 2 Maratha LI of British Indian Army. 5 Division similarly had 9, 10and 29 Brigades with 3 Maratha LI, 2 and 6 Frontier Force (now Sikh LI) 3 Punjab and 18 Garhwal Rifles. On 19 January 41, 4 and 5 Divisions commenced their advance from Kassala with both Divisions advancing along the north and south of the Road Kassala-Agordat. 7 Brigade was sent independently to contact the defenses at Keren from the North.

The roads inside Eritrea were heavily mined. When the British Commonwealth Forces approached Agordat, they found the Italians already dug in and were well prepared to give a stiff fight. In the mean time, 5 Division had bypassed Keru which was held by an Italian Brigade and established blocking positions on the likely route of withdrawal.

When Keru was attacked on 22 January by 4 Division, the Italian defenses there had become untenable. Bulk of 41 Italian Brigade managed to withdraw bypassing the blocks which were established in the east. The commander of Keru defenses along with his staff numbering about 1200 were taken prisoners along with their weapons including some guns. The next battle was for the capture of Agordat.

Agordat was defended strongly with four Infantry Brigades by the Italians. Therefore it was first isolated from Barentu in the South before the attack was launched on Agordat. On 28 January, 14 Punjab and 4 Rajputana Rifles attacked at Cochen Hills, south of Agordat. The defenders reacted violently. Another attack by 5 Brigade along with I Tanks succeeded in cutting off the road to Keren.

Finally the Cochen Hills was captured by 31 January. The Italians withdrew from Agordat leaving behind more than 1,000 prisoners and 40 Guns. In just twelve days, the Commonwealth Forces had advanced nearly 100 miles from Kassala against stiff opposition and heavy mine fields. Similarly, 9 Brigade which advanced from Metamma in the South through Ethiopia also succeeded in reaching their objective.

Keren, the third largest city and a strategically important communication center in Eritrea is located 60 miles northeast of Agordat. After Agordat was captured, the British Forces followed the withdrawing Italian Forces in a hot pursuit. However, the Italians had managed to demolish a Bridge between Agordat and Keren over the Baraka River and mined the riverbed. This delayed the British Forces nearly for 10 hours.

During this time the Italians had reinforced Keren and blew up the shoulders of Fort Dongolaas and Mt Sanchil, blocked the Gorge with debris and laid heavy mine fields there. This was the only major approach by road and rail from the west to Keren. They had also established a road block and covered with fire.

Keren means highland. The highest point is 4300 ft above the sea level. The city is surrounded by high mountains. There were a few gorges between the hills through which Keren could be approached. But most of them were well defended. The hills were covered with thorny bushes which acted like barbed wire. This along with vertical cliff rocks helped the Italian General Nicolangelo Carnimeo to create the perimeter defenses nearly impregnable by the Commonwealth Forces.

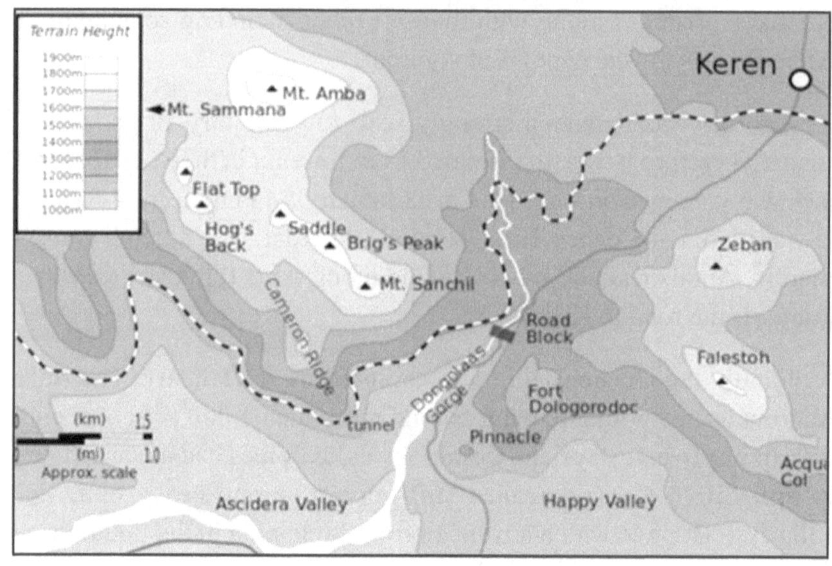

Italian Defenses at Keren

To prevent any further reinforcement, the coastal town of Massama in the east was invested (military tactic of surrounding an enemy town/fort). Initially 4 Division was to capture the Italian positions located in the west of the Road. 11 Brigade of 4 Division was tasked to capture Mt Sanchil, Brig Peak, Saddle, Hog's Back and Flat Top. Mt Sanchil and Brig Peak was to be captured by 2 Cameron Battalion. 1 Rajputana Rifles was tasked to capture Hog's Back. 2 Maratha LI was given the task of capturing the Flat Top.

The attack commenced with 2 Cameron Battalion on 5 February. On the way to Sanchil they captured Cameron Ridge below Mt Sanchil. The attempts made during 6 February to progress the attack towards Mt Sanchil were frustrated by the Italian counterattacks. Many attacks and counter attacks were launched by both sides during the next 10 days around Camoron Ridge.

On 7 February, Indian 5 Brigade attacked Dologorodoc. The plan was to advance through Happy Valley from the south-east, on to Acqua Col and then advance to Mount Falestoh and capture it before final attack was launched on Dologorodoc Fort. 4/6 Rajputana Rifle (now 4 Raj Rif) was tasked to capture Acqua Col. The Battalion launched the attack after last light.

The leading Company Commander was wounded seriously and was evacuated. During the rest of the assault, Subedar Richpal Ram who was the leading platoon commander took over the command of the Company and led the attack.

Richpal and his Company captured Acqua Col and reorganized there by 0430 hours on 8 February. The Italians counter attacked immediately with a large strength and brought down effective fire on Richpal's Company. Richpal's Company repulsed as many as six counter attacks. Finally, since there was no replenishment of ammunition, the Company ran out of ammunition. Having left with no other option under heavy enemy fire, the Company withdrew to their Starting Point.

On 12 February, the second attack was launched on Acqua Col by 4/6 Rajputana Rifles. At 0530 hours Subedar Richpal, now commanding his Company, assaulted Acqua Col. He was injured by an enemy shell. In spite of serious injury in his leg, he encouraged his men to fight and the objective was captured. However, once again he was injured, this time it was fatal. For his exceptional bravery and leadership in the face of enemy, he was awarded with Victoria Cross posthumously on 12 February 1941.

Subedar Richpal Ram

Richpal Ram was born on 20 August 1899 at Barda Village in present day Haryana. He joined the Rajputan Rifles in August 1920 and got his Viceroy Commission in 1936 and became a Subedar. Before his Battalion came to Eritrea he served with the Battalion at Suez Canal area. His Victoria Cross Medal is exhibited in the Rajputana Rifles Regimental Center at New Delhi.

Keren was captured on 27 March after a long hard slugging fight in the most difficult ground and weather conditions. Both sides suffered heavily. Finally when Italians surrendered in April, more than 14,000 prisoners of war were taken. The Battle of Keren was doubtlessly the most important battle of WW II in East Africa. The tenacity and bravery exhibited by the Indian Troops were recognized by the award of two Victoria Cross.

CHHELU RAM AT TUNISIA

Germany began the Second World War in 1939 by attacking Poland. By 1940, most West European countries were in the hands of Germany and her allies. Britain's attempt to contain Germany had not succeeded. To draw out the attention and military resources of Axis Power, the Allies decided to open a new Front in Africa.

For both Allies and Axis Powers, the North African Coast along with the harbors there were strategically important to launch any viable military offensive operations in Africa. Therefore during 1940 to 1943, North Africa witnessed some of the fast moving mechanized and infantry operations. The result of this had major impact on the final outcome of WW II. Large number of Indian Army formations and units participated in the North African Campaign.

The Allies, led by Britain and France, and Axis Power, mainly led by the Italians, had colonized African countries in the East, North and West Africa. At the outset of WW II, the colonial masters were planning to expand their holdings into the neighboring countries. Britain's main interest was to own, control and operate through the Suez Canal to mobilize the resources specially oil from the Middle East countries and other Commonwealth Countries in the Far East. With the increased mechanization of the armed forces, oil had become a strategically important commodity to win any war. To ensure freedom of shipping through Suez Canal, Britain had stationed the Army Units in Egypt. Eritrea, Somalia, Libya and Ethiopia were Italian colonies.

On 13 September 1940, Italian Forces had crossed the Egyptian border from Libya and in three days advanced nearly 50 miles and captured Siddi Barrani (outside the map). The Allies took two months to mobilize their forces and attacked the Italians at Siddi Barrani on 9 December. After having evicted Italians from Egypt, they continued their advance into Libya and by 22 January 1941 had captured Tobruk which is nearly 150 miles from Siddi Barrani.

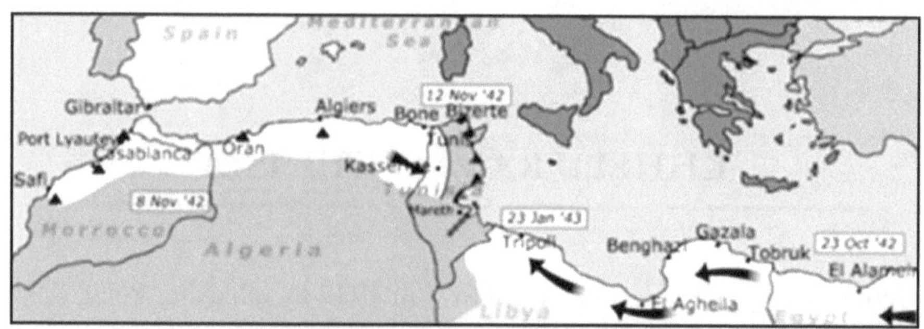

Africa Coast El Alamein to Casablanca

Further advance continued up to El Agehela covering a distance of nearly 500 miles by 9 February 1941. More than 200,000 Italian prisoners and large quantity of arms ammunition and vehicles of various types were captured by the Allies. This operation was known as OP COMPASS. This disaster suffered by the Italians was the main cause of Germans Afrika Korps under General Rommel entering the North African Campaign.

Rommel's Afrika Korps commenced the advance eastwards from El Aghela on 24 March and swept over the thinly held areas in Libya and reached the Egyptian border at Salum on 15 April. However Tobruk was still held by the Allies. Rommel's attempt to capture Tobruk did not succeed. Allies brought in more Forces. The Allies struck back at Rommel and pushed them back to El Aghela on 30 December 1941. The garrison at Salum and Bardia was held by the Axis Forces until the end of January 1942.

Rommel once again commenced his advance towards the East on 21 January. This time he reached El Alamein, deep inside Egypt by July first capturing all the major ports and cities covering a distance of more than 750 miles. At Tobruk more than 30, 000 Allies prisoners were taken by the Germans.

The Allies launched many counter attacks on the Afrika Korps around Alamein without any success. General Montgomery took over the command of 8th Army. With fresh troops, he ordered a major counter offensive known as the Second Battle of El Alamein on 23 October 1942.

During the first week of November, the Germans began to withdraw. The 8th Army chased the Germans into Tunisia by the first week of February 1943. Meanwhile, more Allied Forces including Americans landed in the West African Coast at Casablanca and Oran on 8 November

1942. They advanced into Tunisia within 12 miles of Tunis after defeating Vichy French Forces in Morrocco and Algeria. This operation is known as OP TORCH.

Rommel reacted to the Offensive from the west and counter attacked the American Army at Kasserine on 14 March. His attempt to turn the flank from the north did not succeed due to lack of reinforcement and fuel for the mechanized forces. The Allies decided to attack the Germans holding Tunisia both from the east and west towards the capital city of Tunis.

4 Indian Division which was part of 8th Army was tasked to capture Djebel Garcia and Enfidaville. Djebel Garcia is located about 20 miles east of seacoast and south of Tunis. It consists of large number of bald broken hills which restricted the use of tanks and made infantry movement difficult. It was held in strength by the Germans with extensive defense works and mine fields.

The 4 Rajputana Rifles was tasked to attack in the first phase of the Brigade attack on the night of 19/20 April 43. While approaching the initial objective, the leading company was held up by the fire of a German machine gun detachment which inflicted heavy casualty on the attacking troops making it impossible to advance further.

The Company Havaldar Major (CHM) of leading Company, Chhelu Ram who was armed with Tommy gun (Thomson automatic short barreled gun) rushed at the enemy machine gun detachment firing his weapon and killed all the members. This cleared the way for the Company to continue their assault, capture their initial objective and gain a foothold for further attack.

CHM Chhelu Ram

CHM Chhelu Ram was injured but with total disregard to his injury he continued the advance with the Company. During the next assault his company commander was wounded. Chhelu Ram attended to his company commander and after first aid arranged to evacuate him. He assumed the command of the assaulting company and reorganized it on the objective to face the German counter attack.

The enemy launched counter attack with automatic fire, mortar bombs and physical assault with infantry. Fierce hand-to-hand fight ensued. Chhelu Ram went around shouting 'no withdrawal, we will advance' and encouraged his men to stand up and fight. The counter attack was repulsed with bayonet charge and stones as ammunition were running low.

During this action Chhelu Ram was once again wounded, this time more seriously. He refused to be evacuated until the next attacking company took over. By then he became weak and died of his wound on the night of 19/20 April 1943. For his utmost bravery, leadership to inspire his men and courage in the face of enemy, he was decorated with the highest bravery award, Victoria Cross.

Chhelu Ram, son of o Chaudhary Jairam was born on 10 May 1905 in Dinod village which is now in Bhiwani district of present day Haryana. He joined the Rajputana Rifles in 1931.

Indian Troops in Tunisia after the Victory

During the final days of African Campaign during WW II, the Allies defeated the German and Italian Forces defending Tunis. Bulk of the German Army was withdrawn to Sicily. Montgomery's victorious 8th Army captured Tunis on 7 May 1943. Simultaneously, the American and French Forces entered Bizerte from the west. The Allies took 125,000 Germans and an equal number of her allies as prisoners.

Thus the Allies had become the sole owners of the North African Coast and ensured their naval and other shipping movements through Mediterranean Sea were safe thereafter. This victory in the African Campaign had also assisted the Allies in their future offensive operations on Italy.

YOUNG KAMAL RAM AT CASSINO

After the fall of Tunis in May 1943 during World War II, the German Afrika Korps withdrew from Africa to Italy through Sicily. The Allies 8th Army under Montgomery and 7th US Army under General Patton followed the Axis Forces and landed on the Southern Coast of Sicily on 10 July 1943. Although the Axis counter attacks were successful at the initial stages, they failed to contain the Allies multiple thrusts by Montgomery and Patton in Sicily. They withdrew from Sicily through Messina-Reggio into southern Italy. By 17 August Sicily was under the control of the Allies.

Italy

Sicily

The Allies followed the German Army through Messina Straits into mainland Italy on 3 September. Simultaneously British Troops landed at the eastern Italian port of Taranto unopposed. However the landing attempted in the west coast of Italy at Salerno by the US 5th Army was fiercely contested by the Germans. In the meantime a few Italian Army Officers had arrested Mussolini and entered into an armistice with the Allies. (The Germans later rescued Mussolini from prison and set him up as a puppet leader of Italy.)

By the end of September, the German Tenth Army commenced their systematic withdrawal from Salerno with strong rearguard actions. Thereafter the Germans decided to defend Italy and created series of defensive lines. To name a few, the Gustav Line, the Hitler Line, the Ceaser Line etc. These well thought out defensive lines by Field Marshal Kesselring were based on natural obstacles and coordinated with deep mine belts and covered with fire. Many fierce battles between the Allies and German Forces were fought across these Defensive Lines in this campaign over many months.

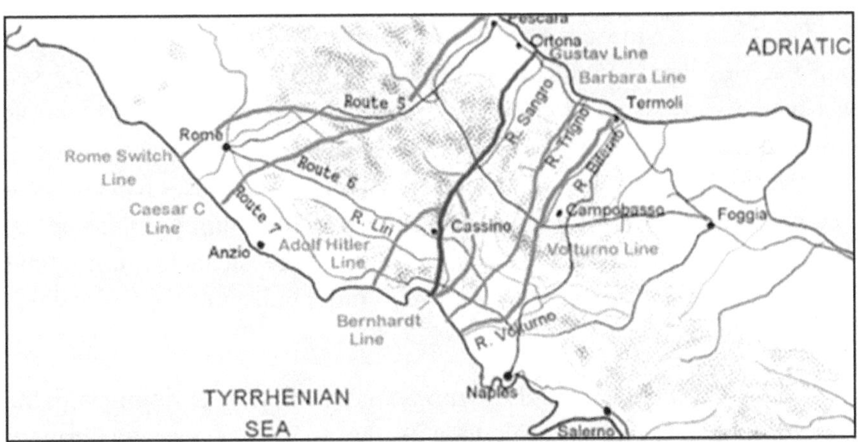

German Defense Lines in Italy

By December 1943, the Germans had retreated to the Liri Valley between Mount Cassino and the west coast south of Rome and occupied Gustav Lines.

Liri Valley

The 8 Indian Division landed at Taranto, Southern Italy moved northwards after crossing Tringo, Sangro and Moro Rivers against German opposition successfully. They decided on a halt short of Gustav Lines to rest and refit during the winters. The Allies plan for the spring of 1944 was to capture Rome, the capital of Italy after penetrating the Gustav Line from the south.

The Gustav Line ran across Italy east to west, coast to coast and along the west bank of the River Gari. From Mount Cassino to the sea coast in the west, it had two more subsidiary defensive lines known as Bernhardt and Hitler Lines. These were the strongest defenses the Allies had confronted since the beginning of WW II. These defenses had concrete bunkers, communication tunnels, gun pits, machine gun emplacements, and shelters to accommodate the infantry and wire obstacles throughout the entire length in conjunction with high mountains and narrow valleys with water obstacles.

Mount Cassino, the highest mountain in this area, dominated the southern approach to Rome along with the main road passing through the Liri Valley effectively. Therefore the Allies planed to capture Mount Cassino before advancing to Rome. Between January and May 1944, the Allies launched three major attacks to break through the Gustav Line Defenses and capture Mount Cassino. All were beaten back by the Germans with heavy casualties on the Allies.

Fresh troops were inducted and trained in river crossing and infantry-tank cooperation and bridgehead battles. The fourth attempt to cross Gustav Line was made during the second week of May. 8 Indian Division was tasked to establish a bridgehead across the Gari River to include Sant Angelo village. Through this Bridgehead Canadian armored brigade was to be inducted and breakout towards Rome. Simultaneously, Gustav Line on either side of Mount Cassino was to be attacked by many other formations to tie down the German reaction.

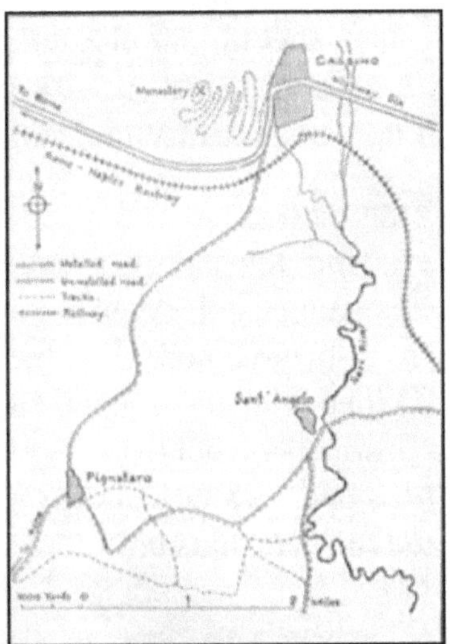

Gari River and Mt Cassino - Gustav Line

The attack was codenamed as Operation Honker. It commenced after a massive artillery bombardment at 2300 hours on 11 May 1944. 8 Indian Division had tasked 17 and 19 Infantry Brigades to establish a bridgehead across River Gari (Rapido) and exploit up to the village Sant Angelo. 19 Infantry Brigade was on the left of the Division Front. The Brigade launched the attack with 3/8 Punjab on the right; left of the center line of the Division Bridgehead and 1st Argyll and Sutherland Highlanders on their left.

River Gari is a fast flowing forty feet wide and seven to eight feet deep river. By 2345 hours the leading Alpha (A) and Delta (D) Company of 3/8 Punjab reached the home bank of the River. The enemy opened up with heavy automatic and artillery fire on them and caused heavy casualty. Though it was a moonlit night, the visibility was reduced to near zero due to German smoke screen which lingered on due to mist.

The leading Companies managed to launch their boats and landed on the far bank. However due to fast current in the River, the boats were swept downstream. This delayed the crossing of the rest of the Battalion considerably. By 0530 hours the Battalion had crossed the River. A and D Companies launched their attack across the German obstacles and managed to gain a foothold. A Company suffered heavy casualty. Only Capt Treman and three more men were left alive. They were taken prisoners. D Company also suffered nearly the same fate.

B and C Company advanced further through the foothold gained by A and B Companies to exploit the initial success of A and D Companies. Their advance was held up by heavy machine gun fire coming from four German machine gun posts.

Sepoy Kamal Ram who himself was under fire volunteered to silence the nearest machine gun post. He crawled under the wire obstacle, approached the post from behind and shot the gunner. The second German, the feeder, was killed with his bayonet. He saw a German officer approaching him with a pistol drawn out to fire at him. Before he was fired at, he shot him dead. Still alone, he attacked the second machine gun nest with grenade and silenced the machine gun.

Sepoy Kamal Ram

By then, more men joined him. He joined with a Havaldar of his Company and they destroyed the third machine gun post. Thus Sepoy Kamal Ram enabled his Company to move forward, launch the attack and capture their objective. His exemplary courage and taking risk beyond the call of duty inspired the others.

Later his Platoon advanced further to dominate the likely approach of the enemy counter attack. They were fired at from a house. Once again brave Sepoy Kamal Ram dashed towards the house and killed a German in his trench. Two more enemies surrendered. His exceptional bravery saved the situation and enabled his Battalion to complete the task assigned to it. For his act of sustained bravery under adverse war conditions he was awarded with the highest bravery medal, Victoria Cross.

Kamal Ram was born on 17 December 1924 in village Bholupura of Karauli district in Rajasthan. He joined 3/8 Punjab during the WW II. He was 19 years old when he was decorated with the VC thus became the youngest Indian to be awarded with a VC. While presenting the VC Medal in 1944 in Italy, King George VI said that it gave him a real thrill to award him his VC. Later he rose to the rank of Subedar and retired from the Indian Army. He died at his village in 1982.

Mount Cassino

In the fourth and final attack across the Gustav Lines, 8 Indian Division successfully completed the task that was assigned to it. Many innovations in river crossing, bridging and infantry–tank cooperation were witnessed during the attacks. Sepoy Kamal Ram was awarded the first VC in the Division in this campaign. All this was achieved at a heavy cost.

One third of the 17 Infantry Brigade were casualties. 19 Brigade suffered somewhat lesser. Mount Cassino was captured and ultimately the Allies entered Rome on 4 June 1944. 8 Mountain Division rightfully earned the reputation of River Crossing Division and their motto became 'One More River'. The Division participated in the Italian Campaign right up to the end and earned many more name and fame.

FEARLESS GHADGE AT UPPER TIBER

During World War II, the Axis Forces were defeated in Africa. They withdrew from Tunis to Italy through Sicily. The Allied Forces followed them. The Allies expected to defeat and destroy the Germans Forces in Italy in a short war. However it did not happen. Hitler decided to give a stiff fight and prevent the Allies from reaching German borders through Italy. To a large extent he succeeded in his plan in delaying and causing destruction to the Allies Armed Forces in Italy in spite of lack of Italian cooperation in his effort.

The mountainous terrain of Italian peninsula was favorable to the Germans to defend Italy in successive Defense lines. Allies 8th Army faced series of river obstacles and Defense Lines while advancing towards the north. The Germans had constructed strong Defense Lines and contested the advancing Army effectively. By April 1944, 8th Army was poised to capture Rome through Liri Valley from the South.

Indian 4 and 8 Divisions were part of the Advancing 8th Army. In addition to 4 and 8 Indian Divisions, the 10 Indian Division under the Command of a British Indian Army Major General DW Reid CBE, DSO, and MC was also inducted into the war in Italy in the Adriatic Sector in March 1944.

Major General Reid was a war experienced General. On reaching the plains of Italy he got down to training his Division for the impending operations. Based on the lessons learned in the Italian operations by the other Divisions and terrain obtained in the projected operational areas, he issued training directives. He emphasized on the need for proficiency in patrolling, river crossing and infantry-tank cooperation. After the fourth battle of Cassino, 10 Indian Division was relieved by 4 Indian Division for advance training in mountain warfare.

Indian 10, 20 and 25 Brigades were part of 10 Indian Division. After the mountain warfare training was completed the Division was tasked to advance towards the Gothic Line defenses astride the Tiber River. It involved series of river crossing, fighting in the low hills and capturing numerous Italian villages well fortified and defended by the German Army.

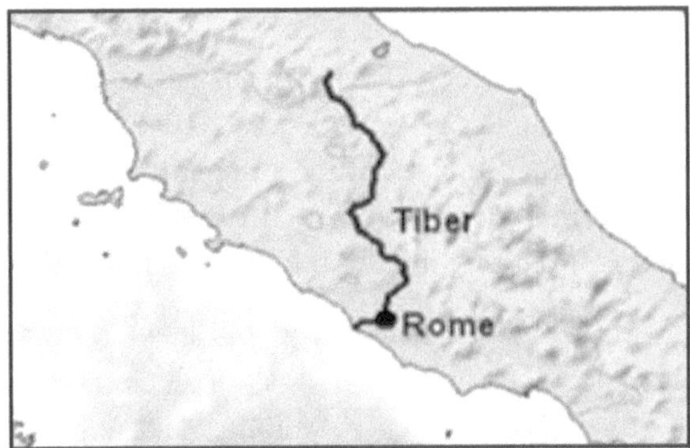

Tiber River

Tiber is a major river passing through the plains of Central Italy in north south direction connecting many important cities and towns. In the upper reaches it passes through narrow valleys flanked by sharp and high hills. The Italian plains are dotted with clusters of villages around castles. In the North, it enters into the mountains. On either side of the River run motor able roads. The Germans had reinforced the area opposite 10 Indian Division in 1944 after the fall of Mount Cassino with fresh troops from the German 305 Division.

10 Indian Division had planned to advance with 10 Brigade to the west of the River Tiber, 20 and 25 Brigades on the east. 20 Brigade was on the right flank of the Division advancing with 8 Manchester 2/3 Gurkhas and 3/5 Marathas. The Marathas, while taking over the advance from the previous Frontier Force Battalion suffered enemy artillery shelling on one of its Company HQ in which the Company Commander and a few others were killed. Presumably the Germans were aware of relief taking place. Other Battalions of the Brigade also suffered similarly.

Having had an unfortunate start, the 3/5 Marathas (Now 5 Maratha LI) had decided to employ their professionalism in their future operations more prudently. The Battalion had devised a method to advance based on the possible enemy reaction and the ground conditions. The terrain was such that a well trained enemy like the Germans could hide themselves, observe the attackers and bring down accurate and devastating fire on them.

Against this 3/5 Marathas had decided to carryout outflanking maneuvers with self contained troops for over 48 hours and cut off the enemy from behind. Historically Marathas have been employing this tactics from the time immemorial.

The advance commenced on the fifth of July. The first obstacle the Brigade confronted was River Grande. By the evening the same day this River was crossed against minor opposition. Thereafter, the 3/5 had followed an outflanking movement to reach behind Monte Falone successfully and captured the objective with very few casualties.

By 7 July the Brigade had advanced and cleared up to Montone, an important German defense node and had taken 65 German prisoners there. On the night of 7th, 3/5 outflanked yet another German position from the north through steep mountain slopes and crashed into the unsuspected Germans who were about to launch a counter attack on the captured locality. In an unplanned skirmish the Marathas with their war cry echoing in the mountains spoiled the German counter attack and rushed towards Monte Falcione, at the hilltop and captured it. Further advance took them to Morlupo.

On the following day, two companies of Marathas attempted to reach the crest of Monte Marucchino. They were able to close in with their objective. However the alert Germans had the wind of the approaching Marathas and opened murderous fire from the top of the hill. Simultaneously the Germans launched a counter attack on the Marathas forward post which was captured earlier and retook the Posts at Point 624.

The Brigade HQ had asked 2/3 Gurkhas to assist Marathas to stabilize the situation. The Gurkhas were on their way. However the Marathas not wanting to give more time to the enemy decided to launch a quick attack to push back the Germans before they reorganize themselves on Point 624.

The Marathas closed in with the Germans without any support fire. The Germans opened up with machine gun from their nests and swept the attackers to the earth at close range. The Company commander and many NCOs and men were killed. One of the section commanders was NK Yeshwant Ghadge. During the attack all his section men were either killed or severely wounded.

Undaunted by the grave situation, he decided to silence the murderous machine gun. He advanced towards the machine gun emplacement and

Nk Yeshwant Ghadge

lobbed a grenade which damaged the machine gun and killed the gunner. Then he single handedly reached the machine gun emplacement firing his Tommy gun on the enemy at point blank range and emptied his magazine killing one more of the enemy. Two were still alive and there was no time to change the magazine. He held the barrel of his gun in both hands and jumped on the enemy and using his Tommy gun as a club he beat two Germans to death.

While he was literally on top of the Germans, he was mortally wounded and fell across the bodies of the enemies he had killed and died. The Company succeeded in capturing the objective. Nk Yeshwant Ghadge saved his Company with his life. The courage shown by Nk Yeshwant Ghadge under a known adverse situation was exemplary. For this act of bravery and self sacrifice Nk Yeshwant Ghadge was decorated with the highest Bravery Medal, the Victoria Cross.

Yeshwant Ghadge was born on 16 November 1921 in Maharastra. He joined 3/5 Marathas in Africa where he was Mentioned in Dispatches in the Battle of Keren. He died on 10 July 1944 when he was just 22 years old.

10 Indian Division under Major General Reid was one of the finest fighting formations which had done proud to the Indian Army. They had fought numerous battles in the mountains and across the rivers to reach Gothic Lines and participated in Operation Grapeshot. The Division was awarded many medals for individual bravery including VC and many

battle honours to the units. The Division Commander was awarded with Companion of The Most Honourable Order of the Bath (CB), a title and order conferred to British and Commonwealth citizens in recognition of conspicuous service to the Crown. On the occasion of Victory Day Celebration on 13 May 1945, the General Officer Commanding Major General Denys Reid gave this message of thanks giving to all members of the 10 Indian Division.

10 INDIAN DIVISION

Apna Kamandar Major General D.W. Reid C.B.E., D.S.O., M.C. ka

KHAS PAIGAN

Main ne abhi Hazur Badshah Salamat aur Wazir i Azam ki paigam sun lie hain. Ap ne sunna hoga kih woh chahte hain kih hain shukriya ada karke aur ziyada taqat laari men lagaen.

Is men koi shak nahin hai kih ham aise namune dekhte hue apna pura hissa lenge.

Aj ham sab log apne mandir, masjid, gurdware ya girje men jama'a ho kar apne mazhab ke mutabiq Itahadion ki bara fatah ke lie Khuda ka shukriya ada karte hain. Ham aise shukrguzar hain kih ham is larai men kamyab ho chuke hain ta kih rahim, dostana aur insaf dunya men qaim rahen.

Har shakhs ko apne dil men saf malum hoga kih jo fatah hasil hua woh apna pura taqat lagane se hua ya nahin.

Abbi irada rakhen kih sulah hasil kar ke hamari sab khiyalat aur kashishen apas men khub samajh o madad qaim rakhne par lagaye rahen. Samajhen kih mel milap aur qurbani ke bughair achcha qaim rahne wala zamana nahin ban sakta hai

Shukriya ada karta hun kih is Division ko itne sile mil chuke hain aur abhi ham log is sulah ke tewar manane ke lie mauqe par hain.

Ham apne sab sathion ko khub yad rakhte hain jo kih larai men kam ae aur zakhmi hue. Ham yaqin karte hain kih unke khandan aur rishtadar in bahadur jawanon ki qurbani se kuchch tasali paenge.

Ap log jante honge kih waqt jald ane wala hai jab is Division ko purah ki taraf jana hoga. Us waqt ham apne bahut sare Birtanwi bhaion se alag hojaenge. Yihi admi jo kih hamare pakke sathi banne rahe.

Isi mauqe par main in ke lie Khuda hafiz, khush qismati aur izzat chahta hun.

10 Indian Division ne is Itali larai men jo nihayat achcha kam kia hai isi kam ke lie main ap sab logon ka khub shukrguzar hun.

Mere ane par jaisa meigh ko ek bana hua Division mil la waisa dusre kisi kamandar ko nahin mil saka. Is par meri khush qismati thi. Thore i kamandaron ko aisi achchi dosti aur wafadari bataji hui hogi jaisi mere ko pahunchte hi ap logon ne batayi.

Ap logon par bahut bhari aur mushkil kam waqt par waqt lagaye gaye. Chand martaba yih waqt na wajib the aur kam namumkin malum hua. Kai logon ne etraz kia hoga magar yih etraz mere kanon tak nahin gahunche.

Ap ki is wafadari, dilchaspi aur hosle ke sabab se main dil se ap logon ka shukriya ada karta hun. Ap log kabhi nahin jante honge main ap ke lie kitna shukrguzar hun.

Chunanchi ap aur main apne Division jo kih ham 15 mahinon se jante hain alwida karenge.

Ap logon tarh se us zamane ko koi nahin bhulega. Is zamane kki ap sab log izzat karenge aur mere se ziyada iski koi izzat nahin karega.

Ap ko sab khush qismati hasil ho aur ap ka main shukriya ada karta hun. Chahta hun kih Khuda 10 Indian Division ke sab jawanon ki khub hifazat kare.

Denys W Reid

C. M. F.
Sunday, 13 May, 1945.

G. O. C.
10th Indian Division

GORKHAS IN ITALY

During World War II more than 25,000 soldiers of Nepali origin (Gorkhas) served in 40 Gurkha Rifles (Infantry) Battalions under the British Rule. Most of them were part of British Indian Army organized on the same lines as the other Indian Infantry Battalions. There were 10 Gorkha Rifle Regiments serially numbered from 1 to 10, each Regiment with two Battalions in the beginning of WW II. Later, more Battalions were added.

Gorkhas participated in all theaters of WW II and earned thousands of bravery awards. This is the story of two brave Gorkha soldiers who fought gallantly and sacrificed their life in Italy during WW II. They were given the most prestigious bravery awards. Their memorials are in the Gorkha War Cemetery at Rimini in Italy.

Rifleman Sher Bahadur Thapa was serving with 1/9 Gorkah Rifles (GR) in Italy during 1944. 1/9 GR was under 5 Infantry Brigade in 4 Indian Division. In September 1944, 5 Brigade was ordered to attack San Marino on the East coast of Italy. San Marino was an independent state surrounded by Italy. The township is located on the western slope of a Hill. Although San Marino was a neutral country, it was forcibly occupied by the Germans. Therefore the Allies attacked San Marino as part of their Italian offensive.

There were two dominating Knolls, Point 343 and Point 366 ahead of the main Town. These two features had to be captured before the main attack on the Town could be launched. After a stiff battle Gorkhas had captured Point 323 on the night of 18/19 September 1944. Just before dawn 1/9 GR attacked Point 366. The leading section commander and Rifleman Sher Bahadur Thapa charged one of the enemy posts on the way to Point 366 and captured it.

The Germans withdrew but soon counter attacked. The counter attack was repulsed. During the ensuing fight the Section Commander was wounded. Sher Bahadur led the attack further on to Point 366 and captured the Knoll after exchange of fire. He reorganized his section on the top and held on there waiting for the reinforcement.

For the next two hours, reinforcement did not materialize. The Gorkhas on top of Point 366 were without ammunition and were subjected to enemy fire. They were in the open and enemy counter attack was building up. They were forced to abandon the Knoll which Sher Bahadur had captured. During withdrawal, Sher Bahadur stayed behind and covered the withdrawal till the last man cleared the crest. Before he abandoned his position, he rescued two of his wounded comrades from the reverse slope. While finally clearing the crest to join his Company he was killed by enemy automatic fire and he died there on 19 September at a young age of 20.

Rfn Sher Bahadur Thapa

This fearless Gorkha was instrumental in saving the life of many of his comrades and prevented major counter attack on the exposed men of his Company. Ultimately his exploits had resulted in the capture of San Marino. For his exceptional bravery, Sher Bahadur Thapa was decorated with a Victoria Cross posthumously. His VC Medal is displayed in the 9 GR Training Center.

There was yet another episode of exceptional bravery by a Gorkha soldier in Italy at Monte San Bartolo in the Central Italy in November 1944. To assist the neighboring Polish Corps on the right, Indian 8 Division was asked to capture Monte Bartolo. The Division tasked 17 Indian Brigade to attack Monte Bartolo. First Battalion of 5 Gorkhas led the advance towards the Brigade objective.

While the leading platoon was crossing a Ridge short of the Battalion objective, the enemy had brought down fire on the advancing Gorkhas from an unexpected position. The Gorkhas were caught in the open. From their position they could not engage the enemy, therefore the Company Commander ordered the Company to withdraw.

To engage the enemy while the Company was withdrawing, Rifleman Taman Gurung ran up to the sky line and engaged the enemy with his gun and threw grenades. Part of the Platoon withdrew to safety. Taman Gurung once again ran up to the skyline with more grenades and engaged the enemy to facilitate the withdrawal of the others from his Platoon. More men could withdraw to safety. One more section was still pinned down under enemy fire.

This brave Gorkha ran up to that section, took the Bren Gun with two magazines and for the third time he went up to the skyline and engaged the enemy from there. He emptied both magazines. By then, the pinned down section also withdrew. However, Taman Gurung was killed before he himself could withdraw to safety.

Thus this brave heart had made almost a deliberate sacrifice of him and exposed him to certain death. For his ultimate sacrifice for the honour of being a brave soldier, Rifleman Taman Gurung was decorated with the highest medal of gallantry, the Victoria Cross posthumously.

Rfn Taman Gurung

Taman Gurung was the second Victoria Cross winner from 8 Indian Division in Italy. By the end of Italian Campaign, 8 Division had a total of four Victoria Cross medals and 4 and 10 Indian Divisions had one each.

WAR BEYOND SENIO RIVER

Towards the end of 1944, World War II was tilting in favor of the Allies who had employed their combined Commonwealth and American military and economic might in Italy. By March 1945, after hard slogging matches, the Allies had captured important Cities of Rome, Perugia, Luca, Florence, Pisa and San Marino. They had attempted to break through the Gothic Defense Line which ran from coast to coast through the Apennine mountains between Florence and Bologna and to the Adriatic Coast south of Rimini.

At this stage priority was shifted to conclude the war in Europe. To achieve that aim a large amount of Allied Forces from Italy were shifted to European Theater. This had weakened the force level of the Allies in Italy.

The Allies had inducted additional forces and managed to breach the Gothic Line defenses at a few places. But they failed to break out from there into the Lombardy Plains towards the north due to adverse winter conditions. As against this, the German Army in Italy was also facing fuel shortage for their mechanized forces.

Notwithstanding the fuel crisis, the German Army made the Allies fight for every inch of Italian territory. The Allies halted their Forces south of Gothic Lines and adopted a strategy of offensive defense while preparing for a final attack when better weather and ground conditions arrived in the spring.

The Allied Forces comprising the US Fifth, British Eighth Army and Brazilian Expeditionary Forces were poised to cross the Gothic Lines on a broad front across the northern Italy in their final offensive before the World War II was concluded by April 1945. Opposing them were the German 10th and 14th Army.

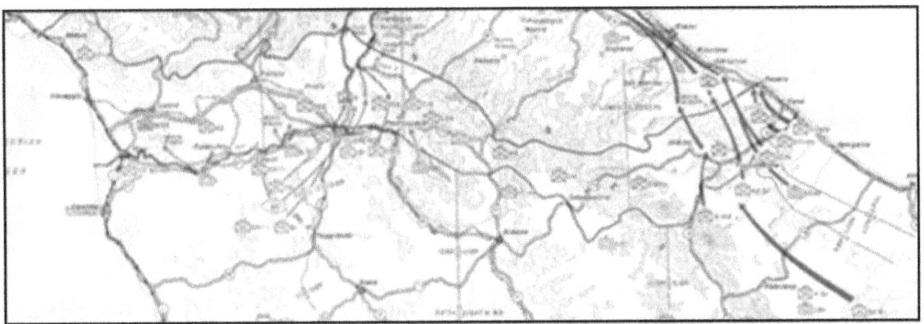

Opposing Forces on the North and South of Gothic Line in 1945

The Eighth Army comprised 5 and 13 Corps which was deployed in the East. The US Fifth Army was deployed to the west. 8 Indian Infantry Division under 5 Corps with its 17, 19 and 21 Infantry Brigades was deployed south of River Senio. On their left was 2 Newzealand Division.

The enemy had his main defensive positions between the Senio and Santerno Rivers. The Eighth Army's plans was to advance and assault River Senio on a broad front, cross the River and establish a bridgehead large enough to launch bridges across the River. They would then break out towards north to destroy the enemy south of the River Po. The 8th Indian Division and the New Zealand Division were the front assaulting Divisions between Lugo and Fusignano.

The Senio is a tributary of the river Reno in the eastern Italy. By itself the river was not a major obstacle to infantry or mechanized forces. But the Germans had converted both the banks of this river into a formidable fighting line. More than 10,000 labourers for over many months were used to create fortified machine gun bunkers, fighting trenches, communication trenches and living areas with overhead protection against direct bombardment on both banks. The banks on both sides were raised varying from 20 to 40 feet high. It could withstand both artillery concentrations and air attacks for hours. The banks were mined and demolition charges were placed.

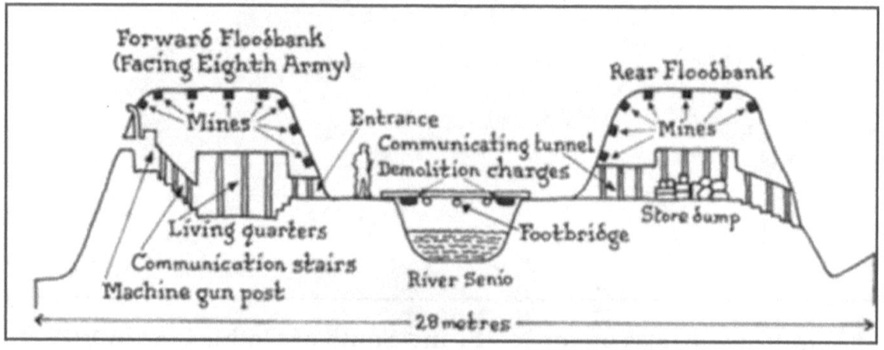

Side view of the Senio River Bank

Front view of Senio River Bank

The 8 Indian Division which was inducted through Taranto in September 1943 had made a name for itself in Italy by conducting successful operation across many rivers through Southern and Central Italy at Cassino and Upper Tiber Valley and had won a VC for bravery. After resting through the winter of 1944/45, 8 Division was ready for a hard fight. 21 Indian Brigade under Brigadier BS Mould had 1/5 Maratha, (Now 1 Maratha LI) 3/15 Punjab and 1 Jaipur Infantry in the lead.

Operation commenced on 5 April with diversionary attacks to keep the enemy guessing about the main offensive along Gothic Lines. On 9 April the bombers dropped large number of fragmentation bombs followed by heavy concentration of artillery fire for over four hours. This was followed by flame throwers such as Crocodiles and Wasps throwing their 100 feet long fearsome jets on the enemy.

The Infantry Battalions closely followed the artillery barrages and flame throwers and attacked on the near bank of the River. The Germans survived the hard drubbing they suffered for over four hours and opened murderous machine gun fire from the bunkers on the 1/5 Marathas. The Battalion suffered heavy casualty including in which the commanding officer and intelligence officer were killed. Three of the Company commanders and many others were wounded.

Against the stiff opposition the leading men of the Marathas reached the far bank. They were subjected to intense machine gun fire. Sepoy Namdeo Jadhav who was the Company messenger, (Runner) in spite of enemy fire, was running around passing messages to forward platoons and companies. While returning, he saw two of the Marathas wounded and lying unattended. He helped them to safety and later evacuated them for treatment through the river. The enemy was firing at the Marathas who were struggling to cross the water and reach the far Bank.

A German machine gun opened up not far from where Namdeo was standing and many of his comrades were getting killed. He decided to avenge their death. With total disregards to his safety he attacked and silenced the machine gun post. Then he climbed up on top of the far Bank and shouted the Maratha War Cry and waved at the remaining men to cross the far bank to safety. Guided by his war cry large number of Marathas crossed the far bank and captured their objectives. Thus he saved many lives and enabled the battalion to secure the bridgehead area. For his supreme act of bravery he was decorated with a Victoria Cross.

Sepoy Namdeo Jadhav

On the same day, 17 Brigade crossed the river adjacent to 20 Brigade to establish the Division bridgehead. 6/13 Frontier Rifles was tasked to establish the initial bridgehead across the Senio River near Fusignano which would be enlarged by other units later. After the intense bombardment 6/13 Frontier Rifles commenced the attack against heavy opposition. By midnight 9 April only three men of 6/13 Frontier Rifles had reached the far Bank. One amongst them was Sepoy Haider Ali, a brave Pashtun from Kohat of North Frontier Province.

Sepoy Haider Ali

Without any orders, Sepoy Haider Ali asked two other comrades to provide covering fire while he moved forward and attacked the nearest machine gun post single handedly and killed the enemy and silenced the machine gun. He was wounded. However, he further advanced towards another post which was about 30 yards away and destroyed the post with grenades killed the enemy there. He himself received serious wounds on his legs.

Encouraged by his success, the rest of the Company reached his location and later captured their objective. By then Haider Ali was bleeding profusely. He was evacuated to safety and was given treatment. He survived his injury and was awarded the highest gallantry award, Victoria Cross for his outstanding bravery. He was the only Pathan who was awarded VC during this War. Later he became a Subedar and retired.

With the success in the initial phase of the operation across River Senio by the 8 Indian Division, the rest of the Eighth Army advanced swiftly towards Po Valley. By 23 April 1945 after fighting many tough battles, Eighth Army reached the Po River. By then the American Army also moved forward. Overall the Germans were retreating in all fronts.

Finally the Italian Campaign came to an end on 2 May 1945 with the signing of the Instrument of Surrender by the German General Heninrich.

By their deeds and sacrifice, Kamal Ram, Taman Gurung, Sher Bahadur Thapa, Yeshwant Ghadge, Namdeo Jadhav and Haider Ali made known to the rest of the world armies that Indians made a great soldier wherever they were sent.

JAPAN SWEEPS SOUTH EAST ASIA

In 1939 Germany attacked Poland. Soon other countries joined the War either with or against Germany. This War which was fought between Allies on the one hand and Axis Power on the other was coined as World War. Later it was known as the Second World War. Britain, as the primary member of Allies, had focused her attention towards Europe to contain German offensive there.

Japan signed an anti-communist pact with Germany in 1937 and a Tripartite Pact in 1940 with Germany and Italy and joined the Axis Power. This enraged the Americans and British. They cut off the oil supply to Japan. Japan was badly in need of oil and other material resources for her ongoing war with China and to fulfill her ambition of establishing a greater Japanese Empire.

In 1940, the Japanese Army attacked Indochina which was ruled by Vichy French Government and occupied it. Later in 1941, they swept through Thailand, Malaya, Singapore and Hong Kong using their army, navy and air force. Next to fall was the oil rich East Indies (Indonesia). Britain did not have adequate resources to defend her far eastern colonies; therefore the Japanese nearly had a cake walk when they attacked the British Colonies and captured them.

Japan wanted to annex Burma (Myanmar) in search of oil and other mineral resources. Besides Burmese resources, Japan wanted to cut off the Burma Road leading from Burma into China and deny the supplies which was being brought into China from Rangoon and used against Japanese Army there. Burma under Japan would also protect her flanks for the defense of newly acquired colonies in South East Asia and act as a base for the future offensive into India.

Burma became a major province of British India from 1886 and remained until 1937 when it became an independent colony of Britain and assumed direct rule there. Large segment of nationalist Burmese were against British rule and were fighting for freedom. 17 Indian Division of British Indian Army and 1 Burma Division were located at various places in Burma under Lt Gen Thomas Hutton. They were organized and mostly employed in internal security duties.

The Japanese Navy attacked Victoria Point in the south of Burma in mid January 1942. They captured some of the strategically important airfields by 18 January against feeble opposition. On 22 January 1942, Japanese Army attacked from the west through Thailand and reached Moulmein and captured it by 31 January. Troops of Indian 17 Division retreated leaving behind large quantity of stores.

While withdrawing, an important bridge over Sitting River was demolished before the troops were able to cross the River. This delayed the crossing of the River and the units of 17 Division had to fight a pitched battle with the advancing Japanese. In this battle 17 Division was nearly annihilated. Large quantity of stores was left behind on the eastern side of the River. Japanese Army pursued 17 Division west of Sittang River. Rangoon was attacked in February 1942 and by 6 March it was under the control of the Japanese Army.

Expansion of Japanese Empire

The Chinese Expeditionary Forces were inducted into Burma in an effort to check the advance of Japanese north of Mandalay. However with reinforced army and air force elements, Japanese speeded up their advance into Central Burma and Mandalay was captured. The underground Burma Independence Army assisted the Japanese against the British and caused havoc in the rear areas of the withdrawing Burma Corps and Chinese Army.

The Allied retreat was impeded by the hoards of civilian refugees, poor road communication, hot and humid climatic conditions and most of all by the onslaught of malaria which caused more casualties in Burma than the Japanese Army. Similar fate was suffered by the Chinese Expeditionary Forces in the North and east. By the end of May 1942, the Burma Corps retreated to Imphal in India.

The Japanese halted their advance at Chindwin River during the Monsoon. In the western Province of Arakan on the Coast of Bay of Bengal, Japanese had advanced up to the Indian border in the Chittagong Hill Tracts. This led to a panic situation in Chittagong. In anticipation of a possible Japanese attack on Chittagong, everything that might be useful to the attacking army if and when they captured the city was destroyed.

Though the Japanese never attacked Chittagong, this scorched earth policy triggered a famine in Bengal in 1943. By mid 1943, it appeared that the Japanese would establish a Greater Japanese Empire in South East Asia. If it did not happen, it was due to a formidable combination of Indian Troops and Generals like Slim who were determined to prevent it from happening at all costs.

PRAKASH SINGH AT ARAKAN

After the fall of Singapore, Malaya, Indonesia, Thailand and part of Burma by mid 1942, the next target of the Japanese Army was possibly Eastern India. The British Indian Army which was stationed in Burma had retreated to India. Following the retreating 17 Division on their heels, the Japanese Army was poised to cross the Indian Border and attack anywhere between Chittagong and Kohima.

General Wavell was the Commander-in-Chief of India. Rather than waiting for the Japanese to attack India, he decided to launch a limited counter offensive into Burma within the limited resources available to him at that time. His aim was to recapture some harbors in western Burma Coast and airfields close to the Indian border to facilitate naval operations and use air power in subsequent operations into Burma to provide logistic supports to the future operations.

The nearest harbor and airfield from the Eastern India were located at Akyab Island in the southern tip of Arakan along the west coast of Burma. From there, the Allied Air Force could operate and support ground operation in and around Rangoon. The plan was to launch an amphibious attack on Akyab Island combined with a ground advance through Mayu Peninsula. The operation was code named as OP CANNIBAL.

Amphibious resources required for launching the offensive operation could not be mustered in time. Therefore the amphibious assault was abandoned. Indian 14 Division with additional resources was tasked to advance along the Mayu Peninsula and capture up to Donbaik located at the southern tip of Mayu Peninsula. From there, Akayab was to be attacked and captured by a seaborne attack.

47 Indian Brigade as part of 14 Division commenced the advance from Cox Bazaar on 17 December 1942. 8 Punjab was part of the advance elements. The advance progressed slowly against stiff enemy opposition.

After delaying the advance for more than two weeks, the Japanese Forces from Mayu Peninsula withdrew to Akyab Island by the first week of January.

On the southern tip of the Peninsula about a mile north of Donbaik, a company of Japanese troops had occupied a delaying position on the beaches between Mayu Hills and waterline behind a tidal creek with steep banks. The defense works were made of timber and sand and was organized to bring down maximum enfilade fire on the beach on the attackers. They were supported with artillery and anti-tank fire.

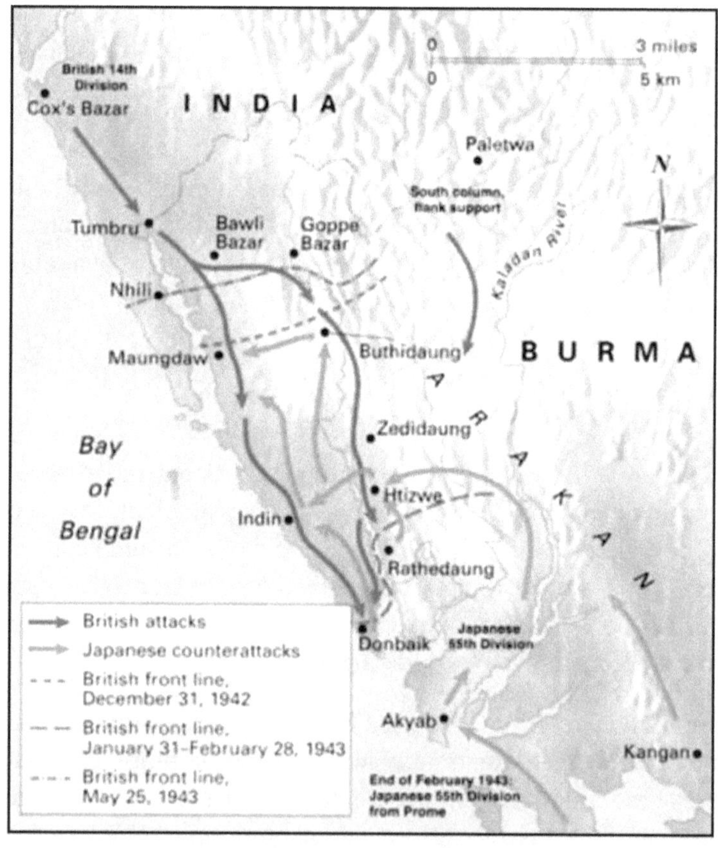

Plan of Advance

8 Punjab which was advancing along the beaches, attacked the Japanese company position on 6 January 43. The attack was repulsed with heavy casualty on the Punjabis. The Japanese brought down heavy artillery fire very close to their own bunkers, causing havoc on the foot

soldiers and had destroyed a few of the Bren Gun Carriers (light armored tracked vehicle with machine gun mounted) of 8 Punjab.

Havaldar Prakash Singh was with one of the Bren Gun carriers. His detachment commander was killed during the attack. Prakash Singh took over the command of the detachment and continued with his task.

Hav Prakash Singh

Bren Carrier

On the beach, he saw that two of the attacking carriers of his Battalion had been rendered out of action by the enemy anti-tank fire. He rushed towards those carriers. Enemy machine gun opened up at him. Prakash returned the fire with his machinegun held with one hand while steering the carrier with the other and neutralized the enemy fire. On reaching the disabled carriers, Prakash found four men lying wounded inside them. He shifted the wounded to his own carrier and took them to safer place for treatment. The attack was abandoned.

Meanwhile, large Japanese reinforcement had arrived in Mayu Peninsula and attacked 14 Division units causing heavy casualty. There was a pause in the battle to reorganize and prepare for further operations. This took nearly two weeks. During this pause, Japanese had strengthened their defenses at Donbaik.

Once again, 8 Punjab was tasked to attack and capture the same Japanese Company position at Donbaik. The attack was launched on 19 January with additional carriers. This time Havaldar Prakash Singh was the Bren carrier commander. During the assault, the Japanese had knocked out many Bren carriers with accurate fire from their anti-tank weapons. One of them went in flames.

Having seen this, Hav Prakash Singh moved his carrier to a safer position. From there he observed the enemy and engaged them. At that time one of the carriers in which his Battalion Officer Lieutenant Bert Causey was leading the attack had broken down due to enemy fire.

Prakash moved out from his safe place towards the immobilized carrier under enemy fire and found Lt Causey and one more man inside the carrier. He realized that both were seriously wounded and would endanger their life if he moved them to his own carrier. Lt Causey told him to leave him alone and go away from enemy fire. Prakash refused to leave them in that condition. With total disregard to his own safety he improvised a tow chain and towed the broken down carrier to safety and saved their lives.

Recognizing the consistent bravery and camaraderie exhibited by Havaldar Prakash Singh under murderous enemy fire on both occasions, his Commanding Officer recommended him for two Victoria Crosses (BAR), one each for his actions on 6th and 19th January. He was decorated with one Victoria Cross for his selfless courage on both occasions.

Captain Parkash Singh VC | Maj Prakash Singh VC with Queen Mother

Prakash Singh was born in 1913 in a village now in Pakistan and grew up to be a good athlete. In 1936 he enrolled in the Army and joined 5/8 Punjab Regiment. By 1943 he became a Havaldar. After the award of the VC in 1943, he was given commission and by 1946 he became a Captain. During the partition in 1947, he joined 16 Sikh Infantry Battalion. He was promoted to the rank of Major and retired in 1968. He died in 1991.

UNIQUE NAND SINGH

Towards the end of 1942, the Japanese had succeeded in their design to conquer most of the Southeast Asian countries including Burma. They were consolidating their gains and preparing to launch their offensive into Indian Territory from the East. The coastal Arakan state of Burma was to serve as the launching pad for the attack on Imphal and Kohima.

To thwart the offensive preparation of the Japanese Army, an attempt was made in December 1942 by General Wavell, the then C in C of India to contain and evict the Japanese from Burma. Accordingly 14 Indian Division launched the first of Arakan Campaigns. The advance commenced on 17 December. Donbaik, the southernmost tip of Mayu Peninsula was attacked on 01 February. It did not succeed. Another attempt was made on March 15 which also ended in failure.

By end of March 1943, the Japanese launched a counter offensive and attacked the British Indian Army positions on either side of Mayu Ranges and captured the strategically vital Maungdaw-Buthidaung road by the first week of May. By then Lieutenant General Slim had taken over the operations in Arakan as 15 Corps Commander.

In spite of many violent counter attacks against the Japanese Uno and Tanahashi Forces, the Allied Forces were not able to hold on to their gains made earlier and had to be withdrawn before the onset of Monsoon in May 1943. The causes of failure in Burma were studied and remedial measures were undertaken before the Allies launched their next offensive into Burma in January 1944.

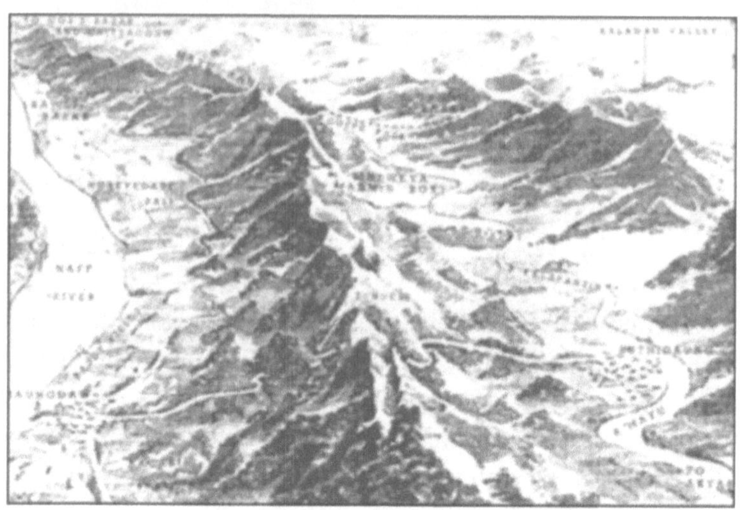

Mayu Ranges – Arakan Burma

The Mayu Ranges are a series of sharp conical hills in north south direction covered with thick jungles and dominate Mayu River Valley and Naft River valley on both sides effectively. Lateral movement is difficult. The only road between the two Valleys which connects Maungdaw with Buthidaung passes through tunnels. Roads are available in north South direction along the rivers.

The offensive under the overall command of Slim commenced in January 1944 with 5 and 7 Indian Divisions advancing on both sides of the Mayu Ranges. Maungdaw was captured by 5 Division on 9 January. 7 Division after having advanced down the Kalapanzin Valley had established their Administrative areas at Sinzweya.

The Japanese counter attacked the units of 7 Indian Division. Their tactics was based on small multiple groups infiltrating deep into enemy defenses, isolate the units and destroy them in piecemeal. Against this well known Japanese tactics, General Slim devised a method in which the isolated units were to group together, organized into a defended area and stay put fighting a prolonged defensive engagements. These defended areas were named as Boxes. These boxes were administratively supported by air and well stocked with ration and ammunition providing them with prolonged staying power.

The Japanese attacked the 7 Indian Division's HQ on 6 February and infiltrated through the Administrative area with a view to attack and capture the urgently needed ration and medicines stocked there. The HQ withdrew to their Administrative area. Together this area was made into an Admin Box. For the first time the units located at the Admin Box withstood the prolonged attacks and fought against the Japanese thus defending the Admin Box successfully in what became known as the Battle of Admin Box. Although the Admin Box was still holding out, the Japanese resumed their advance with a new Division towards Tiddim during the first week of March 1944.

During their advance the Japanese had attacked and captured an important post held by 1/11 SIKH (now 4 Mech Inf) which was guarding the Maungdaw-Buthidaung Road. Having captured it, they had reorganized the defense of the post with well dug foxholes, machine guns and held it with a platoon worth of Sakurai Forces. The Post dominated the main road. With the loss of it the defenses of 1/11 Sikh became untenable.

The task of counterattacking and recapturing the Post was assigned to 'A' company of 1/11 SIKH. The counter attack was launched on 11/12 March 1944. Naik Nand Singh who was familiar with the layout of the Post was leading the assault along the steep ridge which was the only feasible approach to reach the enemy trenches on the top of the hill. Progress was very slow as they had to move one behind the other under enemy fire.

Nand Singh was in the lead and was wounded by the enemy fire. Notwithstanding the multiple injuries suffered by him, he rushed ahead of his section firing his weapon and killed one enemy in an open trench nearest to him. Further he crawled forward and captured a trench single handedly killing the occupant with his bayonet. By then he was severely injured and most of the other members were either dead or wounded.

Painting - Depicting the Attack by Naik Nand Singh

With utter disregard to his safety, he reached for the next trench under enemy fire and killed the enemy and captured the trench. By then the following section was able to reach the top and close in with the enemy to capture the rest of the trenches and foxholes in the post. Thus 1/11 SIKH achieved an important victory due to the courage and bravery exhibited by Naik Nand Singh in capturing three trenches and leading the way to success in the operation. For his act of exemplary gallantry, Naik Nand Singh was awarded with the Victoria Cross.

After the end of WW II, Naik Nand Singh was promoted to the rank of Jemadar and served with 1 SIKH. 1 SIKH was the first Indian Army Unit to land at Srinagar airfield after the accession of Jammu and Kashmir with India on 27 October 1947 to defend Srinagar against the Pakistani Raiders. The unit was part of the Indian Army units which saved Srinagar.

Nk Nand Singh and his mother

Lord Wavell with Nand and Kamalram VC

On 12 December 1947 1 SIKH was tasked to clear the Raiders from Uri Area. The Battalion cleared the Raiders by destroying their bases and was returning to Baramulla. On their way back, the Battalion was ambushed by the Raiders in which Jemadar Nand Singh VC was killed while counter attacking the Raiders. He was awarded with a MVC for his exceptional bravery in the attack posthumously. Thus Jemadar Nand Singh became a unique Indian who was awarded two bravery awards, a VC and a MVC.

Nand Singh was born on 24 September 1914 at Bahadur Village, Patiala State, Punjab and joined the 1/11 SIKH on 24 March 1933. He won the highest bravery award from Britain and the second highest Indian bravery award. A bus stand has been named after Nand Singh at Bareta Town in Punjab known as Shaheed Nand Singh Victoria Bus Stand. His statue has been put up in Bathinda at Fauji Chowk.

THE VC BATTALION

Many Infantry Battalions from the six out of ten Gorkha Rifle Regiments of the British Indian Army took part in the Burma Campaign during World War II. During the retreat from Burma and later advance into Burma, all the British Indian Army Brigades had at least one Gorkha Rifle (GR) Battalion in their order of battle.

The Gorkhas proved themselves as ferocious jungle fighters and earned many awards for bravery including nine Victoria Crosses. One out of them, 2/5 GR, received three Victoria Crosses and distinguished itself as the largest number of VC winning Battalion in Burma.

5 Gorkha Regiment was raised in 1858 as 25 Punjab Infantry Battalion and later was re-designated as 5 Gorkha Rifle Regiment in 1901. The Regiment participated in WW I and II and in Afghan Wars. During WW II the 2nd Battalion of Five Gorkha Rifle Regiment (2/5 GR) was part of 48 Infantry Brigade which joined the 17 Infantry Division at Bilin River.

The Japanese 33 Division had launched a multi pronged attack on the weak 17 Division and forced it to withdraw across Sittang River. 2/5 GR was detailed to fight the rear guard action for the withdrawing Division to delay the Japanese advance.

The withdrawal of 17 Division commenced from Tiddim on 15 Mach 1943 with Japanese 33 Division in a hot pursuit. By the third week of May, leading elements of advancing Japanese had reached the base of Chin Hills and had occupied some tactically important features on Basha East Hill. Retaking these features was important for delaying the Japanese advance.

One feature dominated the road and provided good observation over a long distance. It was a tall sharp feature with narrow approach which precluded the use of large body of troops to attack. Therefore priority was given to attack that feature with a platoon. Against the well prepared defences of Japanese, the attack did not succeed. Another attack was launched which did not make any headway either.

Burma

On 24 March a third attack was launched. This time it was with more troops. Havaldar Gaje Ghale was commanding the leading platoon consisting of young and motivated men. While advancing to the objective, Gaje and his platoon came under fire. He rallied his men and encouraged them to move forward under murderous fire from the well prepared Japanese trenches.

Although he was wounded, he did not bother about it and he, along with his Platoon, closed in with the enemy trenches. There was a bitter close quarter fight with bayonets and Kukhris. Grenades were used liberally and many Japanese inside their trenches were killed. With loud Gorkha war cries reverberating in the hills and display of indomitable courage the objective was captured with heavy casualty on both sides. The platoon which followed Gaje Ghale's platoon moped up the enemy and reorganised there. Only after that Gaje agreed to be evacuated to dress his wounds.

Havaldar Gaje Ghale

For this act of exceptional bravery and leadership qualities exhibited by Havaldar Gaje Ghale in the face of the enemy under adverse circumstances, he was awarded the highest bravery award, the Victoria Cross. With that, Gaje opened the VC account of 2/5 GR. The VC Medal was presented to him at Delhi by the Viceroy of India.

While 17 Infantry Division was withdrawing along the Tiddim-Imphal Road to the plains of Imphal, Japanese 33 Division made many attempts to prevent 17 Division from reaching Imphal intact so that this Division was not available for the defence of Imphal. However, the Division reached eventually after three weeks of intense fight and suffered more than 1,500 casualties. At the plains of Imphal, 17 Infantry Division was deployed in the area of Bishenpur, south of Imphal along the road leading to Silchar. 2/5 GR occupied many important defended posts in and around Bishenpur area to prevent the Japanese from infiltrating into the plains of Imphal and guard important logistics centres located there.

Subedar Netrabahadur Thapa of 2/5 GR was commanding a platoon-defended post located on a prominent hill known as Mortar Bluff at Bishnpur. It was an important post for the security of Bishenpur. There were two other posts, one each on either side. One was about 400 yards and the other was closer. The closer one on the south was attacked and captured by the Japanese on the night of 24/25 June 44.

On 25 June, the Japanese had been firing at the Mortar Bluff intermittently. At about 1830 hours, the Japanese brought down heavy volume of fire on the Post. After some time, a Japanese company attacked the Post. The Gorkhas fought back fiercely.

Subedar Thapa moved from trench to trench and exhorted his men to fight back. Not a single trench was lost. After a fierce fight Japanese withdrew leaving behind their dead and injured. Thapa reported the matter to his Commanding Officer and asked for additional artillery support which was promised.

Sub Netrabahadur Thapa

It had begun to rain. Taking advantage of rain and darkness, the enemy once again attacked the Post from a different direction. The section which came under attack was unfortunate to have their Light Machine Gun breaking down. The enemy captured that section and was preparing to exploit further.

Meantime, Subedar Thapa readjusted his defenses and contained the enemy from further expanding. His commanding officer suggested to him that in view of large casualty his Platoon had suffered, he could withdraw from there. To that he requested for reinforcement with additional ammunition and said that he would defend the Post and evict the enemy from there. The CO agreed and sent a section of troops with additional ammunition.

However, the reinforcing section was intercepted by the enemy and all became casualty. Notwithstanding the tragic situation, Subedar Thapa gathered the ammunition brought by the unfortunate reinforcement section and distributed it among the men still left in the post and urged them to fight.

He and his men fought the attacking enemy bravely with grenades and hand-to-hand with Kukhri and did not give away another yard of ground. The attempts made by the enemy to run over the Post were frustrated. While fighting, Subedar Thapa had suffered a bullet injury on his face. Later, a grenade exploded above him killing him instantaneously. His dead body was found with his Kukhri still in his hand and a few heads of Japanese detached from their body close to it.

For his outstanding act of bravery and the ultimate sacrifice he made, he was awarded with the Victoria Cross posthumously. Thus Subedar Nethrabahadur Thapa had contributed one more VC to the Battalions' VC Account.

For 2/5 GR, 26 June 1944 was a day full of Blood and Fury. Many of their Posts scattered around the vital military installations around Imphal were under attack. It appeared that the Japanese were desperately trying to create an opening into Imphal to capture the badly needed food supply and medical stores there. One platoon of C Company, 2/5 GR help an important post known as Water Post on Silchar Road which had two strong points 200 yards away from each other but were mutually supporting.

The Japanese attacked that Post and captured it. Considering the tactical importance of the Post, C Company was ordered to recapture it. On 26 June the Company launched an attack. Naik Agansing Rai with his section was leading the attack. When C Company reached the top of the hill feature, the enemy opened up with machine gun fire on them. In the absence of any cover from the enemy fire, Naik Rai decided to rush his section towards the enemy in the open rather than waiting to neutralise the enemy fire before the assault. Any delay would have resulted in more casualties.

Naik Agansing Rai

Rai led his section in an assault on the enemy trenches covering nearly 50 yards in the open and killed three Japanese soldiers in the first trench. Encouraged by the initial success, the rest of the attacking Gorkhas charged and captured the first strong point.

Having captured the initial objective, Rai led the rest of the platoon against enemy heavy machine-gun fire coming from the second strong point and rushed forward with a grenade in one hand and a Thompson sub-machine gun in the other. Having reached the position, he and the rest of his section killed the occupants of bunkers with grenades and Tommy-gun fire. The remaining Japanese fled into the jungle.

Thus C Company recaptured their Post nearly at the same time when Subedar Netrabahadur Thapa had frustrated the attack of Japanese with his life on the Mortar Bluff Post. Naik Agansing Rai was awarded a Victoria Cross. It was a Red Letter day in the History 2/5 GR in which two VCs were won on the same day.

The Trio of the VC Battalion

After India got her independence, 2/5 GR remained with India. Havaldar Gaje Ghale was promoted to the rank of Honorary Captain and retired from the Indian Army in 1964. Naik Agansing Rai retired in the Rank of Subedar.

2/5 GR with three VCs in their credit had rightfully earned the name of VC Battalion.

IMPHAL - THE SPRINGBOARD TO VICTORY

The fighting all around its (Imphal) circumference was continuous, fierce and often confused as each side maneuvered to outwit and kill. There was always a Japanese thrust somewhere that had to be met and destroyed. Yet, the fighting did follow a pattern. The main encounters were on the spokes of the wheel, because it was only along these (roads) that guns, tanks, and vehicles could move.

- General Slim

Imphal, the present day capital city of Manipur, is an important communication centre in the northeast of India located about 70 miles west of Indo Burmese Border. During World War II, Imphal witnessed some of the fiercest large scale decisive battles around the town. It is located in a bowl of about 75 km diameter of plain area surrounded by thickly forested high hills.

During early 1940s many roads and tracks from different directions converged at Imphal. An all-weather metal road connected Imphal with Kohima and a track from Iril River Valley, both from the north. Other roads were from Ukhrul in the northeast, from Tamu in the east, from Tiddim in the south and from Silichar/ Bishenpur in the west.

Due to good connectivity, many advance military bases and depots including airfields were located in and around Imphal. Thus it became a strategically important focal point for the Allies to defend and for the Japanese to capture it. Loss of this town to the Japanese would have ended the Burma Campaign in victory to the Japanese and would have been the end of their dream to get back Burma for the Allies. It would also have impacted the ongoing operations in the northern Burma and the Chinese operations against the Japanese in China.

Having realised its importance of defending the Imphal Plains, General Slim, the 14th Army Commander, decided to guard the Town and the military facilities in and around there at all cost. Divisions were moved to be deployed all around the Town. So great was the importance and urgency of defending Imphal, that 5 Indian Infantry Division was moved by air and deployed in the north of Imphal.

By the beginning of 1944, Imphal was strongly defended from all directions. 20 Division at Tamu was guarding the eastern approach, 23 Division was deployed in and around Imphal and 17 Division at Tiddim defended the approach from the south. In addition, 50 Para Brigade and 254 Tank Brigade were also available for the defense.

The 15th Japanese Army under General Mutaguchi planned to capture Imphal in an operation codenamed as U GO. The major fighting units were from Japanese 31, 33 and 15 Divisions. A diversionary attack was launched in Arakan before launching the main attack on Kohima and Imphal. The Japanese crossed the Chindwin River on 8 March 1944 and contacted all the three Divisions guarding Imphal Plains.

In the north, Japanese 15 Division attacked and captured a supply dump at Kanglatongbi on the Imphal-Dimapur Road. The Japanese were disappointed as the supply dump there had been emptied before their attack. Further they captured Nungshigum Ridge which dominated the airfield at Imphal. On March 29 the Japanese had cut off the Imphal-Kohima Road and laid a siege. Now the only route open for the Allies was by air.

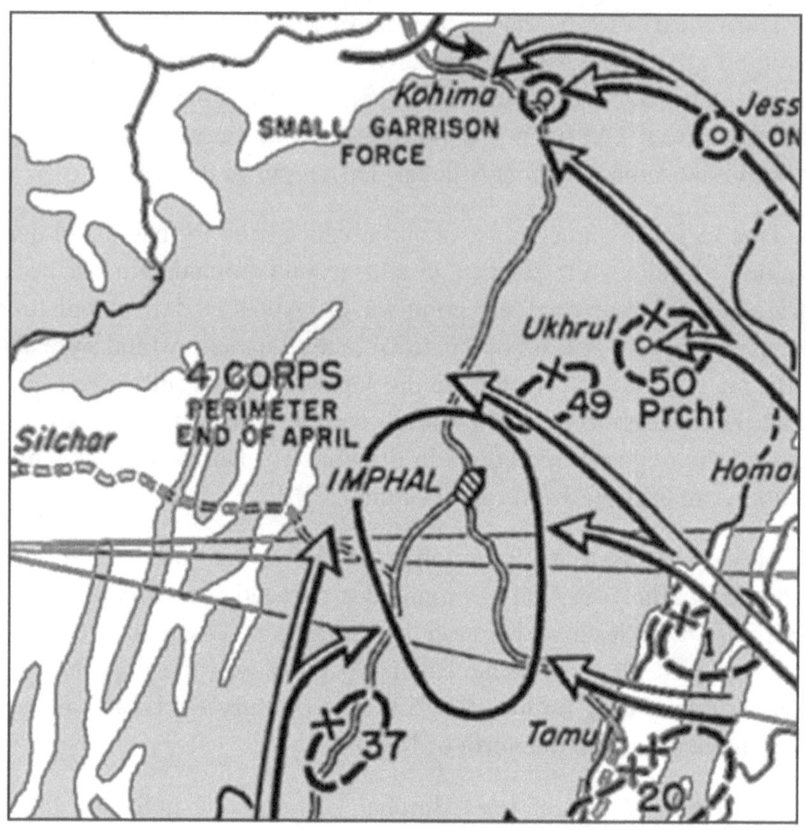

Japanese Attack Plan on Kohima and Imphal

Ferocious fighting ensued between the opposing forces to conclude the battle of Imphal in their favor. In the words of Bill Slim, "The fighting all around its (Imphal) circumference was continuous, fierce and often confused as each side maneuvered to outwit and kill. There was always a Japanese thrust somewhere that had to be met and destroyed. Yet, the fighting did follow a pattern. The main encounters were on the spokes of the wheel, because it was only along these (roads) that guns, tanks, and vehicles could move".

9 Indian Brigade of 5 Division was deployed west of Iril River protecting the Imphal-Kohima Road in the north. 3/9 JAT (now 3 JAT) commanded by Colonel Girty was part of 9 Brigade. The Battalion was carrying out extensive patrolling in the area ahead of their forward line of defenses to prevent against surprise attack and provide early warning of Japanese movement if any, by establishing patrol bases.

On 5 April, the Japanese attacked one of the patrol bases of 3/9 JAT on top of a mount about 10 miles north of Imphal. The numerically superior Japanese overwhelmed the patrol base and occupied it in strength. Early morning the next day a patrol was sent to assess the enemy strength and disposition at their erstwhile patrol base. It was reported that about a platoon (40 men) worth of enemy were occupying temporary defense with machine guns. To prevent the Japanese from operating from that patrol base, the Commanding Officer of 3/9 JAT had decided to launch an attack and recapture the mount.

At 0930 hours, a company of 3/9 JAT attacked the Japanese. Abdul Hafiz was the commander of the leading platoon. To approach the objective, the attacking Jats had to negotiate steep climb devoid of any cover. Own artillery provided covering fire during the approach. Hafiz kept his men motivated with encouraging words and led them from the front. The enemy opened fire on the Jats when Hafiz and his men reached the top of the mount.

Without further delay, Hafiz along with his men charged on the enemy trenches. A machine gun which had caused many casualties was firing at him. Hafiz rushed at the machine gun detachment and killed the gunner. Second member of the detachment was also killed by one of his platoon member. Hafiz was wounded. In spite of his injury, he kept up the pressure on the enemy and captured more trenches killing the enemy. Another machine gun opened up from very close to where he was standing. Hafiz lunged at the machine gun and pulled the gun by the barrel. The gunner was shot by a sepoy who following Hafiz. During close quarter fight that ensued, Hafiz was wounded for the second time.

Jamedar Abdul Hafiz

Memorial

In spite his injury Abdul Hafiz led his men in the final phase of the company attack towards the last trench of the enemy and captured it. He continued to encourage his men and inspired them to give their best. After capturing all the enemy trenches, he collapsed on the objective shouting, "Reorganise on the objective... I will give you covering fire". Soon after, he died of excessive bleeding from his wounds. For his exceptional bravery and inspiring leadership during the successful attack, he was awarded the Victoria Cross.

The Battle of Imphal began in the northern perimeter of the Imphal bowl with Japanese attacking against 5 Indian Division and capturing Nungshigum heights. Later the Division had retaken this Ridge from the Japanese and ensured that the airfield at Imphal remained operative throughout the battle. In the east, 20 Indian Division held their 25 miles front with the loss of only two miles when they readjusted their defenses. Southwest of Imphal, 23 Division prevented the Japanese from making any dent in the perimeter. Thus the Battle of Imphal ended in favour of the Allies on 22 June.

The Japanese, having stretched their line of maintenance and failed to capture the badly needed supplies from the Allies Supply Depots located at Imphal, gave up the hope of invading deeper into the Indian Territory and commenced their withdrawal. The defeat at Imphal had cost the Japanese their dream of ruling over the South East Asia and it became a turning point for the Allies in their effort to retake Burma and later the rest of Common Wealth Countries in this region. Indeed, Imphal became the springboard for the victorious Allies Forces during the WW II in South East Asia.

SUBEDAR RAM SARUP AT VITAL CORNER

The Allies came out victorious in the Battle of Imphal and Japanese were forced to retreat into Burma. General Slim ordered his Army to launch an offensive at the heels of the withdrawing Japanese towards the east and south by the end of June 1944. 5 Indian Infantry Division was ordered to advance towards Tiddim. 123 Infantry Brigade under Brigadier Denholm Young comprising 2nd Battalion Suffolk Regiment, 2nd Battalion 1st Punjab Regiment, 3rd Battalion 2nd Punjab Regiment, 1st Battalion 17 Dogra Regiment and 3rd Battalion 9 Gurkha Rifles had captured Tiddim and were heading towards Kennedy Peak.

The leading elements of 123 Brigade had advanced 5 miles east of Tiddim covering a distance of nearly 150 miles. Vital Corner was 8 miles ahead from there. The Kennedy Peak, a massive conical hill feature standing at 8,800 ft (MSL) high dominated the main Road Tiddim-Kalemyo. Strong defenses had been prepared by the Japanese 33 Division in and around Kennedy Peak area to include heights of Salium Vum, Vital Corner, Kennedy Peak and White House which is south of Kennedy Peak.

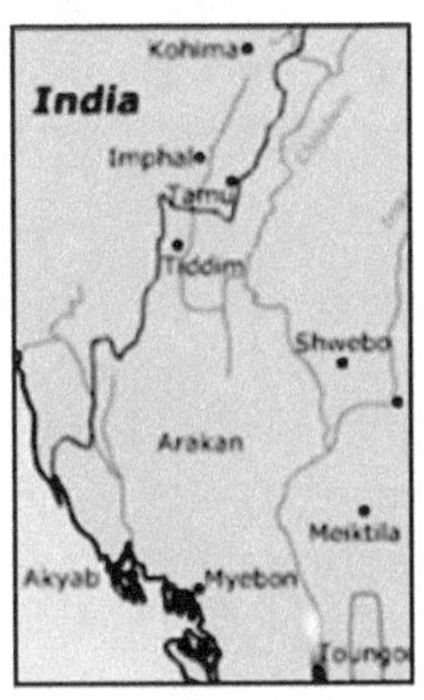

Imphal - Tiddim

Vital Corner - Kennedy Peak

Vital Corner - Kennedy Peak - Kalemyo

The Road was mined and the approaches were blocked with obstacles and road blocks. 3/2 Punjab had occupied Valvum Heights east of Tiddim and captured Point 5955. Japanese counter attacked this position three times and failed to recapture from 3/2 Punjab. They withdrew from there leaving behind their casualties. Salium Vum was occupied by 2/1 Punjab.

The Brigade was preparing for the attack on Kennedy Peak. The likely routes to the objectives were reconnoitered by strong patrols and tracks were constructed. The main road was blocked and Japanese vehicles plying on it were targeted. 3/2 Punjab had captured an Inspection Bungalow which was used by the Japanese, known as Dimlo. The road was repaired and cleared for future use up to one mile short of Japanese held Vital Corner. The Brigade had a fairly good idea of the dispositions of the Japanese defenses as the result of extensive reconnaissance carried out by all units.

In the preliminary phase of the attack on Kennedy Peak, 2/1 Punjab was tasked to capture Salium Vum. On 25 October 1944, 'A' and 'C' Companies attacked from north east from a feature known as Jamshed Hill. At the same time 'D' Company launched a diversionary attack under Major Gian Chand. Before he went for the attack, Subedar Ram Sarup, one of the Platton Commanders of Gian Chand, shook hand with his Company Commander and said, "Sahib, either the Japs or myself today".

Sub Ram Sarup Singh

The main attack was stalled by the murderous fire of the enemy. However one platoon of 'D' Company under the command of Subedar Ram Sarup Singh succeeded in capturing their objective in spite of heavy opposition. Further, Ram Sarup mustered one section of his platoon and led another charge on the nearest Japanese bunker adjacent to his objective.

Completely shocked by the unexpected attack from a different direction by the Gian Chand's Company, the Japanese fled from there. Ram Sarup engaged them and killed many more while running away. He was wounded in both legs. He disregarded his bleeding legs and reorganized his platoon on the objective to face the inevitable Japanese counter attack.

The Japanese counter attacked in waves of about 20 and rained grenades on Ram Sarups Platoon. The Japanese shouted in Urdu saying "don't fire" and demanded from him to surrender. Instead, Ram Sarup collected a few able bodied men and assaulted with machine gun on the attacking enemy. Hand-to-hand fight ensued. He encouraged his men to stand up and fight saying Japanese are not invincible.

Ram Sarup charged a Japanese soldier with bayonet and killed him. Simultaneously he was hit in the chest by a burst of fire. Before he died, he called his Havaldar and told him, "I am dying, but you carry on and finish the devils". Later when volunteers were called to bring in his dead body still under Japanese fire, the entire company volunteered. The gallant action of inspired the entire 'D' Company so much that they were ready to die for him. Such deeds will inspire all the future generations to come.

The Victoria Cross was awarded to Subadar Ram Sarup Singh posthumously for his inspiring leadership and exceptional bravery in that engagement against heavy odds.

Ram Sarup Singh was born on 12 April 1915 at Kheri in the State of Patiala, Punjab. His VC Medal is displayed in Lord Ashcroft Gallery housed in Imperial War Museum, London. His name is engraved in Rangoon War Memorial.

Rangoon War Memorial

After a long and hard fight, the Punjabis stood on top of the Kennedy Peak on 03 November. The Japanese retreated towards the east. Capture of Kennedy Peak cleared the way for the Allies to advance further into the mainland Burma.

BHANDARI RAM AT MAYU RANGES

The Allies entered Burma after defeating the Japanese in the Battle of Imphal at the end of the Monsoon season in1944. 14th Army with 4 and 33 Corps advanced towards the Central Burma. 15 Corps advanced into the Arakans with 25 and 26 Indian Division and 81 and 82 West African Divisions. 25 Division advanced along the Mayu Peninsula southwards for the third time in two years with 51 Brigade covering the eastern slope of the Mayu Ranges. 16th Battalion of 10 Baluch Regiment (16/10 Baluch) was part of 51 Indian Brigade.

While advancing on 22 November 1944, the leading company of 16/10 Baluch commanded by Major Usman Khan came under fire from a Japanese delaying position located at a dominating hill. The leading scouts were killed. The Company halted to clear the enemy. The Japanese delaying position was about 80 feet higher than the surrounding hills; the two sides of it were nearly vertical.

The enemy was guarding the other two sides strongly with machine guns. The approach to the enemy position precluded conventional attack in any assault formation. Having appreciated the situation Major Usman decided to send a selected team of four men to climb up to the top from the vertical side and destroy the enemy and resume the advance at the earliest. Sepoy Bhandari Ram and three other tough men were chosen for the task.

Bhandari Ram led the team and started the tough climb on the vertical face of the Mount. Having reached midway, he lowered a rope for the others to climb. While climbing further up, the Japanese sniper spotted them and brought down fire on them. Unhurt, they moved further. Having reached the top, they crawled towards the enemy trenches taking advantage of thick undergrowth on top.

They were spotted and Japanese fired at them. Bhandari Ram who was in the lead was injured and the other three were killed. Having realized the precarious situation, Bhandari Ram feigned as if he was dead. Japanese who came out to check the dead bodies believed all four were dead and returned to their trenches.

Sepoy Bhandari Ram VC

After some time when he was able to muster his energy, Bhandari decided to avenge the death of his comrades and crawled towards the enemy. When he reached about 15 feet from the enemy, he saw the trench nearest to him was a machine gun trench which was occupied by three Japanese. He closed in further stealthily, stood up and lobbed a hand grenade into the machine gun trench. The grenade exploded killing all three. He quickly pulled out the Japanese machine gun and fired at the enemy rushing towards him. Four more Japanese were killed.

Bhandari Ram was seriously wounded and bleeding. He was happy to see more men of his company had reached the top of the mount before he fainted due to excessive bleeding from his smashed leg and other multiple injuries. Having cleared the mount, the Company resumed the advance. Bhandari Ram was evacuated for treatment. After treatment at various Military Hospitals he was given a long convalescence leave in his village.

For this unprecedented bravery of a young Sepoy and persistent fighting spirit with determination, Bhandari Ram was decorated with the Victoria Cross. The VC medal was presented to him by Lord Wavell, the then Viceroy of India on 9 March 1945 at Delhi.

Bhandari Ram was a subject of Raja Anand Chand, the then ruler of Bilaspur State in the present day Himachal Pradesh. Raja honored Bhandari Ram by escorting him to Delhi for the award ceremony in his own Royal Coach and on return held a Reception in his honor. He was also presented with one thousand silver coins and 10 acres of land.

Wavell presenting VC

Hony Capt Bhandari Ram VC

The Baluch (originally Balooch) Regiment had its origin in the former Madras Army. Sir Charles Napier had raised this Regiment. During WW II as part of British Indian Army, the battalions of 10 Baluch Regiment had Hindu Dogras and Muslims serving together. Since Independence, Baluch Regiment forms part of Pakistan Army. After partition, Bhandari Ram joined the Dogra Regiment and retired as Honorary Captain in 1969. He died on 19 May 2002.

GOOD GUNNER UMRAO IN KALADAN

It is the sacred duty of every gunner to defend his gun;
if need be with his life.

- Anon

During World War II, defeat of the Japanese Forces at Kohima and Imphal was the turning point in Burma Campaign. The Japanese victory runs came to an end. Now it was the turn of Allies to defeat the Japanese in detail and evict them from Burma. The Allies 14th Army under General Slim was made responsible to destroy the Japanese Forces in Central Burma and re-occupy the country.

General Slim had planned to advance his Army to Mandalay in the Central Burma with 4 and 33 Corps. 15 Corps was to advance and destroy the Japanese in Arakan and capture Akayb by the end of January 1945 and contribute to the success of 14th Army. Accordingly 25 Indian Division was ordered to advance and clear Mayu Peninsula, 82 West African Division (WAD) was to advance in the Kalapanzin Valley and 81 WAD further west down the Kaladan River Valley. 26 Indian Division with 3 Commando Brigade was to capture Akyab Island.

15 Corps commenced its preparations in September 1944. Based on the earlier experiences, the Corps units were reorganized keeping in view the terrain obtained in Arakan, the type of operations to be conducted and the need for uninterrupted and efficient logistic support. The units were made self contained in animal transport. Mechanical transports were reduced. Artillery units were placed under command of each Division.

81 WAD was tasked to advance down the Kaladan Valley to Myohaung simultaneously with the 25 Division and 82 WAD towards Akyab. 33 Mountain Artillery equipped with 3.7 inches Howitzer under Major IMG Williams was allotted to 81 WAD and had to undertake a long and tough march over two weeks to join 81 WAD on 21 November. During this period they were maintained by air. The advance commenced on 12 December 1944.

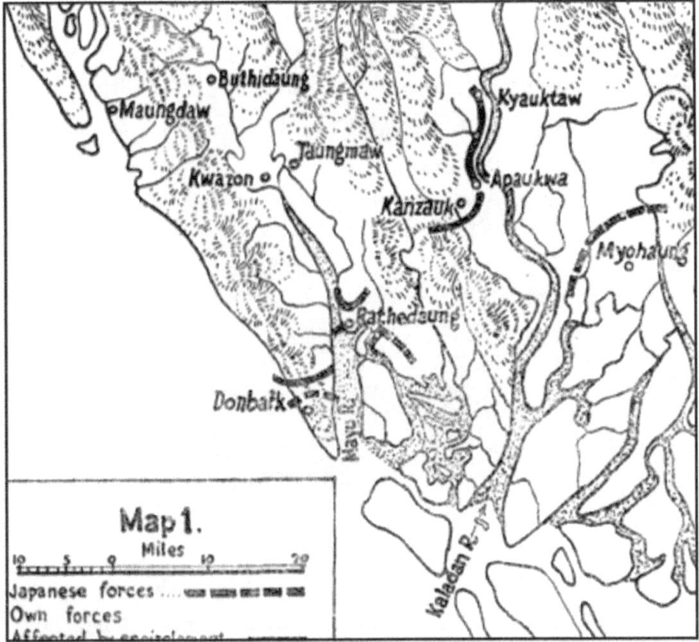

Map - Arakan Kaladan River Valley and Mayu Peninsula

The Japanese stay behind parties frequently interfered with the advance of 81 WAD in small groups forcing frequent halts and imposing considerable delay. Bypassing them was more time consuming due to the nature of the terrain. The Japanese employed hit and run tactics to tire the advancing troops. They also frequently brought down artillery fire on the leading elements.

The artillery guns were therefore grouped with the advancing brigade used to be deployed on the ground to engage the Japanese artillery guns/mortars whenever they opened up on the advancing troops. They used to follow the method of leapfrogging to ensure continuous cover to the advancing infantry. The protection of the gun positions used to be ensured by the infantry brigade. This method speeded up the advance to some extent.

On 15 December, 8 Gold Coast Regiment was leading the advance under 5 WA Brigade. During the advance the Japanese opened fire on the leading platoons of 8 Gold Coast. In a quick counter attack the 8 Gold Coast cleared the opposition forcing the enemy to run away leaving behind the dead body of a Japanese officer.

During the night 15/16, the Battery less one section was deployed in the Divisional Area. Lt VN Mathew was the commander of the forward gun position. The local protection to the forward gun position was provided by 8 Gold Coast Regiment. Havaldar Umrao Singh was the detachment commander of one of the guns.

Hav Umrao Singh

Around 2100 hours, the Japanese brought down heavy artillery shelling in the Divisional area. It lasted for an hour. Lt Mathew ordered counter bombardment immediately. At 2200 hours the Japanese attacked and penetrated the outer protective ring of the 8 Gold Coast Regiment and reached the Forward Gun Position. The 8 Gold Coast fought bravely but could not isolate the Gun Position from enemy attack. When the Japanese attacked the Gun Position, Havaldar Umrao Singh and his detachment occupied the trenches which they had prepared earlier and returned the fire on the enemy. They were able to hold the attack twice but most of the gun detachment was either killed or seriously injured to fight back except Hav Umrao Singh. He was also injured.

Once again Japanese attacked. This time Umrao, armed with his section Bren Gun, killed the attacking Japanese and protected his gun which is more dear to any gunner than his life. After the Japanese withdrew, he searched the Gun position for someone to reorganize the defense of the guns. He found two who were able to stand up and fight. There was not enough ammunition left with them. Between them, they decided to save the Gun at all cost.

The fourth attack on his gun came after some time. The three returned the fire at the attacking enemy with the few rounds of ammunition they had. All three including Umrao were injured. Now Umrao was alone standing next to his Gun. He had no ammunition left to fire. He picked up the gun bearer (a long iron rod used for supporting the gun barrel while it is unscrewed) and attacked the enemy with it and killed three of them. With total disregard to his safety and to save the Gun from the last of the attackers he charged and killed him. Then he collapsed and fell down next to his Gun.

Painting - Hav Umrao Singh Attacking the Japanese with a Gun Bearer

Early morning the next day, when the Gun Position was searched, Umrao Singh was found next to his gun badly injured but still breathing. His gun bearer was still clutched in his hand and a few Japanese dead bodies smashed badly were lying near him. It was estimated that about two companies of Japanese had launched the attack on 8 Gold Coast. Umrao Singh's gun was intact and it was put to use for firing immediately.

Umrao was evacuated and treated for multiple bullet and shell injuries. After a long treatment he recovered and rejoined his Regiment. The personal example set by Havaldar Umrao Singh has no parallel in the history of the mountain artillery gunners the world over. His supreme example of devotion to his Gun and exceptional gallantry had convinced King George VI to present a Victoria Cross Medal personally at Buckingham Palace on 15 October 1945 for the first time and the only time to an artillery gun commander. Jemadar Surat Singh of the same unit was awarded the IDSM for bravery in this action.

Umrao Singh was born in village Paka near Rohtak in Punjab (Haryana) on 21 November 1920. He joined the Army in 1939. Before he retired in 1965, he was promoted to the rank of Subedar Major (Hony Capt).

Hony Capt Umrao Singh VC

There is an interesting anecdote which took place when Hony Capt Umrao Singh VC visited London in 1995 to attend 50th Anniversary of Victory in WWII at Westminster Abbey. After the function was over, he came out of the Abbey and was waiting to cross the road to go to his car park. The UK Deputy Prime Minister, Michael Heseltine halted his car next to him, saluted him and introduced himself.

When Umrao Singh thanked him for inviting him for the function Michael Heseltine replied, "It is we the British who must thank you and the Indian Armed Forces for the contributions made during the World Wars I and II". Further when he was told that his car was holding up the traffic behind his car so he must move ahead, he insisted that the VC holder crossed the road first. He waited until Hony Capt Umrao Singh VC crossed the road.

15 Corps successfully completed the task assigned to it in the Third Arakan Campaign. By the end of January, the entire Arakan and Akayab Island were recaptured. With that the Allies could fully concentrate on the Central Burma and the race to Rangoon.

JEMADAR PRAKASH ACROSS IRRAWADDY

The longest opposed river crossing attempted (at Irrawaddy) in any theatre of the Second World War.

- Bill Slim

During World War II the Japanese attacked Kohima and Imphal after crossing Indo-Burmese border with the intention of annexing the Eastern India with Burma. However, the Indian 14th Army under General Slim had repulsed the attack with heavy losses on Japanese. Due to acute logistic problems the Japanese had decided to withdraw from Imphal back into Central Burma. The 14th Army had decided to chase the withdrawing Japanese Forces, destroy them and recapture Burma. 33 and 4 Corps was tasked to advance and capture Mandalay. 15 Corps was ordered to advance into the Arakans.

33 Corps commenced the advance after Monsoon season by the end of 1944 and crossed Chindwin River at Kalewa. To progress the operation further east across the River Irrawaddy towards Mandalay, the Corps made extensive logistic preparations. General Slim had planned to establish two bridgeheads across the River Irrawaddy to keep the enemy guessing regarding the next objective of the Allies in Central Burma. Accordingly 7 Division from 4 Corps and 20 Division from 33 Corps were ordered to establish two bridgeheads simultaneously.

On the night of 12/13 March 1945, 20 Indian Division crossed the River Irrawaddy about 20 miles west of Mandalay and established a shallow bridgehead at Myinmu. The Japanese counter attacked the units deployed in the bridgehead violently. Initial counter attacks were repulsed. However, the Japanese brought more troops and launched fresh counter attacks one after another. The counter attacks continued for a week.

100 Indian Brigade under Brigadier William Arthur was part of 20 Division which was tasked to expand the bridgehead towards south. 14th battalion of 13 Frontier Regiment (14/13 FR) was deployed in the

bridgehead at Kaulan Ywathit on the eastern bank of River Irrawaddy. The battalion had defeated many counter attacks between 13 and 16 Febraury and expanded its bridgehead gradually. 'A' Company of 14/13 FR was deployed at Kaulan Ywathit with two platoons forward and one in depth. One of the forward platoon commanders was Jamedar Prakash Singh.

On the night of 16/17 March, the Kaulan Ywathit Company of 14/13 FR came under heavy artillery and mortar fire. A little later around 2130 hours the Japanese attacked the two Forward Platoons and closed in with the Right Platoon commanded by Jemadar Prakash Singh. The enemy was engaged with heavy firing from the Platoon.

Prakash Singh moved from trench to trench in his platoon and encouraged his men to stand up and fight. The attack was repulsed. The Japanese withdrew without further pressing the attack. Prakash was injured in his legs and was not able to walk. His company commander ordered him to come to his HQ for treatment. The Platoon second-in command took charge of the Platoon.

A little while later, the Japanese attacked the Right Platoon for the second time. The second-in-command was killed and the Platoon suffered almost one third casualty. Having heard of this bad news, Prakash crawled back to his Platoon locality from the company HQ and took charge of his platoon.

Not being able to walk, he dragged himself and crawled from trench to trench with his elbows to the front line. He found his platoon 2-inch mortar was silent. He crawled up to it and found that both men of the detachment were dead. He asked his orderly to prop him up behind the gun and recommenced firing. His Company commander visited him at the forward locality and found him busy firing the mortar.

Prakash arranged to collect ammunition from those who became casualty and distributed to the others. By 0130 hours, one third of his platoon was killed. One of the machine gun detachment members was killed during the attack. Jemadar Prakash Singh, by now twice injured, dragged himself up to the machine gun trench and started engaging the attacking enemy from an open position as he could not get down into the trench and stand up to fire. The Japanese closed in the trenches and hand-to-hand fight ensued.

Jemadar Prakash Singh

Prakash Singh shouted the war cry so loud that the entire Company was electrified and fought ferociously. The attack was defeated with heavy casualty. The remaining few Japanese withdrew. Prakash Singh was injured once again and was bleeding profusely. He knew he was dying. Before he collapsed, he encouraged his men to continue to remain steadfast and glorify the name of his Unit. He died soon thereafter.

For his conspicuous bravery and ultimate sacrifice of his life, Jemadar Prakash Singh was awarded the Victoria Cross. Son of Udham Singh, from Kanachak near Kathua in J&K, Prakash Singh was born on 01 April 1913. His name is engraved in the Rangoon War Memorial.

Meiktila was captured on 22 March and Mandalay fell a few days after that. This pawed the way to the Race to Rangoon and final victory to the Allies in Burma.

PUNJABIS AT MEIKTILA

The defeat of Japanese at Imphal and Kohima in World War II was the turning point in Burma campaign. This enabled the Allies to pursue the withdrawing Japanese Army and launch counteroffensive to recapture Burma. For the Japanese, the year 1944 ended in a disaster. They suffered another catastrophe during the next year in the loss of Meiktila in March. Thereafter, the Allies commenced their race to Rangoon.

The Allies counter offensive was planned by General Slim's Fourteenth Army with a view to recapture Mandalay and it was code named as Operation Capital. Later it was called Operation Extended Capital when Mandalay and Meiktila were captured earlier than expected and the Race to Rangoon began. The Japanese suffered heavy losses in men and material during their attack on Imphal. However the Japanese units still had a lot of fight left in them.

On the Allies side, the British Army was finding it difficult to replace the casualties suffered by the British Army units which had to fight under the hostile climatic conditions in the malaria-infested Burmese jungle. Consequently, a much higher proportion of Indian Troops had to be inducted in the Operations Capital and Extended Capital.

Road communications were improved and better logistic support was planned based on air supply during the offensive. With the improved logistic lines and enormous resources available to the Allies from Commonwealth Countries and USA, the Allies were able to field a larger Army to evict the Japanese from Burma.

Slim - the Genius of a General - had visualized the impact of change in the geography of the battle field from mountainous jungle to planes as is obtained around Mandalay-Meiktila (Central Burma) on the projected operations. He suitably modified the composition of units and formations HQs participating in Operation Capital. More mechanized elements were introduced and greater battle field mobility in the form of light and medium wheeled and tracked fighting vehicles were inducted. Air support played a vital role.

To prevent the Japanese from moving out of Arakan and reinforcing the formations fighting in Central Burma, 15 Corps was tasked to advance into Arakan to contain and destroy the enemy there.

By November 1944, the Fourteenth Army had established two bridgeheads across Chindwin River. IV Corps broke out from the northern bridgehead with 19 Division leading the advance towards Mawlaik. From there 19 Division was ordered to clear Shwebo and advance towards Mandalay.

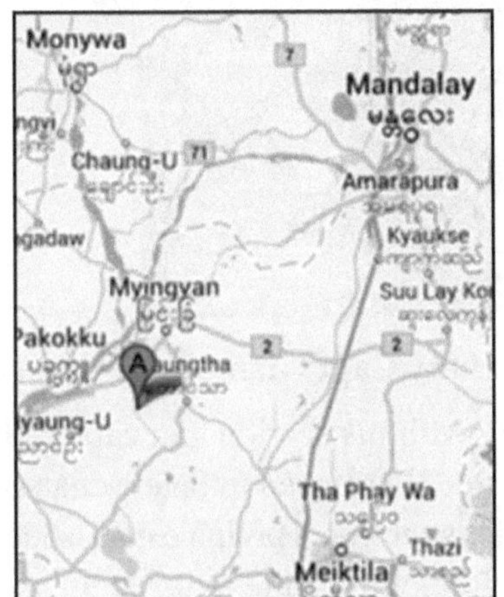
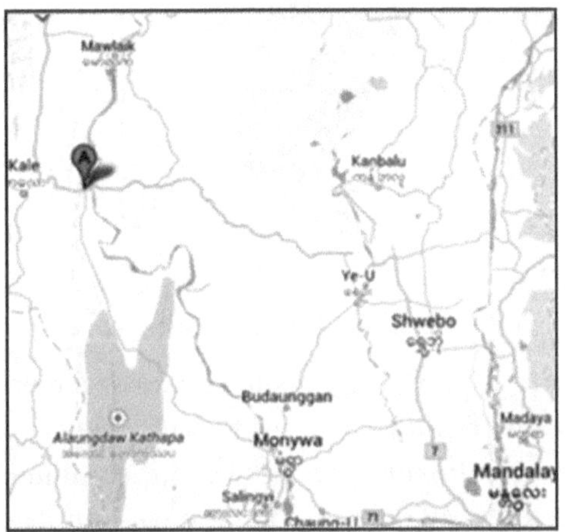

Between Rivers Chindwin and Irrawaddy

The Japanese Army did not give any major fight between Chindwin and Irrawaddy Rivers. Therefore the Allies advanced rapidly fighting against Japanese rear guards. 7 Indian Division advanced through the Gangaw Valley west of Chindwin River under Major General Evans.

The Division comprised of 33, 89 and 114 Brigades. Each Brigade had an identical composition of a British Army Infantry Battalion, a Battalion each of Punjabis and Gorkha Regiment. 4/15 Punjab was part of 33 Brigade. During February/ March 45, the Battalion fought against the Japanese rear guard in many decisive engagements around Myingyan.

On 2 March 1945, 4/15 Punjab was leading the advance towards Myingyan. Naik Gyan Singh was with the leading platoon. While advancing, the leading Company came under enemy artillery fire and encountered a strong Japanese delaying position which had many well camouflaged foxholes.

The Battalion decided to envelop the enemy position with two companies. This was done successfully by sending troops about one and a half miles behind the Japanese position. Main attack was launched from the west. One of the leading sections was commanded by Naik Gyan Singh. When the Company closed in with the enemy they faced heavy automatic fire and suffered some casualties.

Naik Gian Singh

Hony Capt Gian Singh VC

Gyan Singh rushed towards the enemy with his section and captured a few foxholes nearest to him. He was injured. He refused to be evacuated for treatment and continued his command of his section. Having established a foothold, another platoon was launched along with some tanks to attack the enemy from where heavy fire was coming.

While the attack was in progress, Gyan Singh observed some more enemy foxholes had opened up from behind a hedge and were firing at the Punjabis who were attacking the neighboring Japanese locality. He ordered his light machine gun to provide covering fire and he himself firing his Tommy gun attacked the enemy. He threw grenades and silenced the interfering enemy foxhole.

Then he observed that the troop of tanks which was attacking the enemy locality, was about to be fired at by a Japanese anti-tank gun. In spite of his wounds, he rushed towards the enemy anti-tank gun, killed the crew and captured the weapon. His section followed him and mopped up the enemy. Thus own tank casualty was averted.

Later, twenty Japanese dead bodies were found in that area. When he was ordered to go to the Regimental Aid Post to treat his wounds for the second time, he requested permission to remain with his Section till the time the entire objective was captured. He was permitted to continue commanding his section till the end that day.

Thus Naik Gyan Singh by his gallant and successful actions against the enemy enabled the Battalion to resume further advance without undue delay and prevented the enemy from causing heavy casualty on the Battalion. For this consistent and continuous act of exceptional bravery, Naik Gyan Singh was awarded with a Victoria Cross.

17 Indian Division was tasked to attack and capture Meiktila from multiple directions with heavy artillery support, tanks and infantry. Due to lack of anti-tank weapons, the Japanese soldiers were asked to crouch in their trenches with 250 kg bomb and explode the bomb when a tank passed over the trench. However it was not very effective.

By 4 March Meiktila was captured. The Japanese reacted violently and brought in their reserve Division to counter attack Meiktila. By the time the Japanese Division arrived at Meiktila, the Allies were well reorganized at Meiktila and held it strongly. Therefore the Japanese laid a siege and counter attacked the town from the north. They also attacked the airfield outside the town and forced the Allies to cease the air operation from there. The town was maintained by air drops for many days.

The Japanese Army was handicapped by the lack of logistic support and anti-tank weapons. The troops were tired and their morale was drooping. They failed in their counter attacks to recapture Meiktila. They also suffered heavy losses in men and materials. Meiktila remained in the hands of Allies.

Having secured Meiktila earlier than expected, Slim ordered 7 Division to capture Myingyan. The attack was launched on 18 March. With tanks in support, 4/15 Punjab was tasked to attack and capture a strongly held Japanese location at a Cotton Mill outside the Town. The attack commenced with the tanks leading the assault.

Visibility of the tank was masked due to heavy dust. Infantry assault was held up frequently due to frequent halts by the tanks to identify the enemy locality. The tanks had to be guided frequently. Lieutenant Karamjeet Singh Judge was with the leading Company of 4/15 Punjab behind tanks. While following the assaulting tanks the Infantry was exposed to enemy firing during frequent halts. To speed up the tank movement, Lt Karamjeet would go up to the leading tank, indicate the targets to the crew and guide it on to the objective. He repeated this procedure many time under hostile small arms and artillery fire.

In this manner, many enemy bunkers were destroyed and the attack progressed steadily. Later when Karamjeet could not communicate with the tank crew due to noise and thick dust and in the absence of any inter communication, the attack was held up. Exposing himself to the enemy fire, Karamjeet decided to climb up on top of the leading tank to guide the crew to an enemy medium Machine gun bunker which was causing serious casualty on his Company. While climbing up, a burst of enemy machine gun fire mortally wounded him and he was killed instantaneously.

Lt Karamjeet Singh Judge

Tanks advancing to Meiktila

This fearless young officer of 21 years of age, exhibited bravery in successive engagements with the enemy with total disregard to his personal safety and inspired his men, leading them from the front before he sacrificed his life. His action vastly contributed to the success of his Battalion.

Myingyan was captured on 22 March. This led to linking up of Myingyan with Meiktila by rail and the supply line had greatly improved. For his contribution to the success in the attack and sacrifice of his life beyond the call of duty, he was awarded the Victoria Cross. This was the second VC awarded to 4/15 Punjab within twenty days of the first VC awarded to Naik Gyan Singh.

Lt Karamjeet Singh Judge was the son of the Inspector General of Kapurthala State in Punjab. He was born on 25 May 1923 at Kaputhala and joined 4/15 Punjab Regiment in 1944.

Naik Gyan Singh was born on 5 October 1915 at Sahapur in the Punjab. After Independence, he joined the Sikh Regiment and reached to the Rank of Subedar Major and retired as Honorary Captain. He died on 6 October 1986.

The names of all the awardees of VC in Burma are engraved in the War Memorial at Rangoon.

The Allies did not expect to defeat the Japanese in the Central Burma so soon. Having captured Mandalay and Meiktila earlier than planned, Slim decided to race to Rangoon and recapture it before the Monsoon rains set in. 33 Corps advanced along the Irrawady River and 4 Corps along Sittang River and attacked on Rangoon.

The Japanese offered some resistance initially, but they did not have the wherewithal to prevent the Allies from capturing Rangoon. By mid of 1945, Japanese war fighting potential had broken down. They were facing defeat everywhere. Rangoon was finally recaptured by land, sea and air attacks by 02 May 1945 by the Allies.

| Race to Rangoon | Japanese surrender | Rangoon VC Memorial |

Thus the Battle of Meiktila and Mandalay stood out as the last decisive Battles fought by the Japanese Army against the Allies Fourteenth Army which had predominantly Indian Troops and most of all a British Indian Army General led the victory. 4/15 Punjab had the honor of receiving two VCs at Meiktila.

LACHHIMAN GURUNG

Fourth Battalion of 8 Gorkha Rifles (4/8 GR) was part of 89 Brigade under 7 Indian Division when it was Racing to Rangoon in May 1945 during World War II in Central Burma. The Division crossed the River and advanced southwards. By the first week of May 45, 4/8 GR after crossing the River had captured a Japanese Company locality successfully.

On 9 May the Japanese withdrew towards Taungdaw after a few unsuccessful attempts to retake the position. 4/8 GR had sent two companies to cut off the route of withdrawal with a view to trap and destroy the withdrawing Japanese. The Japanese surrounded them and cut off their line of communication. Being encircled, two companies of 4/8 GR organized their defenses and were ready to face the attack by the Japanese.

One of the forward sections was covering the most likely enemy approach of attack along a track. It was a tactically important position. Loss of it would have provided access to the enemy to the company HQ location. Rifleman Lachhiman Gurung was occupying one of the trenches which covered the most likely enemy approach. Gurung was 27 years old and was 4 feet and 11 inches tall. In spite of his overage and lesser height than the standards laid down for recruitment, he was recruited for his physical ability.

Rfn Lachhiman Gurung

On the night 12/13 May 1945, the Japanese attacked the 4/8 GR company along the track where Lachhiman was manning the forward most trench. The section returned the fire. The Japanese closed in and threw a grenade at Lachhiman. The grenade landed in front of his trench and was static. He grabbed the grenade and threw it back at the Japanese.

The Japanese suffered casualty with their own grenade. After some time another grenade was thrown at him that landed inside the trench. Once again he managed to pick up the grenade in time and throw it back at the enemy. When it happened for the third time, Lachhiman was not lucky. Though he had grabbed the grenade, it exploded before he could throw it. He suffered serious injury in his right arm and face. The other two occupants were also wounded.

Unmindful of his injuries, he carried his weapon with one hand and engaged the attacking enemy. Single-handedly, he prevented the enemy from capturing his section locality till reinforcement arrived. The Japanese were not able to break through the defenses in spite of repeated attacks. Finally on the 15th, the Japanese withdrew leaving behind 87 dead bodies.

For the exceptional courage and determination shown by Lachhiman, he was awarded the Victoria Cross. The medal was awarded to him by Lord Louis Mountbatten in Delhi on 19 December 1945. He was given a long treatment at various military Hospitals. But his right hand and right eye could not be saved.

Hav Lachhiman Gurung VC

Lachhiman was born in Dakhani village in Nepal on 30 December 1917. In 1940, he enrolled in 8 Gorkha Regiment. After Independence he was promoted to the rank of Havaldar and retired in 1947. He died on 12 December 2010. One of his sons became an officer in 8 GR.

INDIAN OFFICERS

The future of Indianisation in the Army lies in the hands of the Indian Officers.

- SK Brown, Secretary Military Department in India, 1925

Great Britain, one of the geographically small countries ruled the largest part of the world in 19 and 20th Century. It was said about Great Britain "el imperio en el que nunca se pone el sol" (the empire on which the sun never sets). While the British had a vast empire they had very small native population to govern it. At the same time they were apprehensive of locals rebelling against the alien power.

In the case of India, the British perceived a threat from Russia to their empire in India via Afghanistan in addition to internal rebellions. Therefore, they raised and maintained a vast standing army from the Indian local population and from Nepal but the officers were Britishers. After the Sepoy Mutiny in 1857, the Army in India was taken over directly under the British Government which was earlier functioning under the East India Company.

Until 1920, both the British Army Units and the British Indian Army units were trained, administered and employed by the British Officers. There were very few Indians belonging to the loyal Indian princely families who were commissioned as officers in the British Indian Army prior to 1919. To name a few, Capts Amar Singh, Jodha Jung, Prithi Singh, Malik Mumtaz and Lt Sawai Singh were from the princely families. Though they were trained at Sandhrust in Britain, they had not risen to higher level in command.

The Indianisation of British Indian Army began in 1918 when 25 selected Cadets were admitted in the Royal Military College at Sandhrust. Out of 25 Cadets admitted in the first batch, only 10 had qualified and given commission. Rajindersinghji, Himat Singh, Mahadev Singh and Nathu Singh Rathore were among them who later rose to high ranks in the

Army. The Indian Cadets found it difficult to successfully complete the rigorous training at Sandhrust.

Later to prepare the Indian Cadets for Sandhrust, Prince of Wales Royal Indian Military College was started at Dehradun in 1922. Thus it became a feeder institution to the Royal Military College at Sandhrust and to the Indian Military Academy from 1932. Those who passed out from Sandhrust were known as King Commissioned Indian Officers (KCIO). They were posted to eight selected Regiments and units of the British Indian Army.

To meet the urgent need of officers during the Great War, the Daly College at Indore in the present day Madhya Pradesh was converted into an Officers Training School under General Henry Daly in 1918. The first and the only batch included KM Cariappa, Ponnappa, AA Rudra and many others.

The process of training of Indian Cadets at Sandhrust did not produce satisfactory result. Therefore it was decided to open a parallel Military Academy to Sandhrust known as Indian Military Academy in India at Dehradun in 1932. About 40 selected Gentlemen Cadets each in two batches per year were trained there. Large number of additional Indians were trained both at the Indian Military Academy and Officers Training Academy at Madras during WW II.

By 1939, when World War II started, majority of selected Indian Army units had Indian Officers serving in them. The names of the Indian officers who served in the British Indian Army before August 1947 that stand out are KM Cariappa, KS Thimayya, JN Chaudhuri, PP Kumaramangalam, SHFJ Manekshaw and PS Bhagat. There were others who contributed to the success in WW II (and subsequently to the Indian Army). These were the pillars of the Indian Army when India got independence.

Brigadier KM Cariappa was promoted to the rank of Major General in 1947 which was the senior most rank the Indian officers attained by that time. He had 28 years of service. He was commissioned into Carnatic Infantry in 1919 from Officers Training School (Daly College) Indore. Later he joined the Rajput Regiment. He served in Mesopotomia before he was selected to undergo the Staff College Course at Quetta in 1933 (Present day Pakistan).

Later he served in Iraq, Syria and Iran during World War II. He was deputed to the 8th Army before returning to Hyderabad to raise the 17th Battalion the Rajput Regiment, of which he took command, being the first Indian to be so honoured. He held that appointment for a year after which he was posted to the Eastern Command HQ in Calcutta. From there he was sent to the Arakans in Burma to join the 26 Indian Division under overall command of Lieutenant General William Slim.

He was promoted to the rank of Lt Col and commanded his unit, Queen Victoria Rajput Light Infantry in 1942. Later he served in 26 Division in Burma under General Slim. He was awarded OBE and was Mentioned in Dispatches. In 1946, he was promoted to the rank of Brigadier and commanded Frontier Brigade Group.

Cariappa OBE

Cariappa had achieved many firsts in his career; first Indian to be commissioned at 19 years of age, first Indian to enter the Staff College, first to command a Battalion, first Indian Brigade commander and first to attend Imperial Defense College in London. He was one of the senior most Indian Army Officers on the day of independence, holding the rank of Major General. (Later he was an Army Commander as Lieutenant General, first Indian C in C as General and Field Marshal.)

Another well known officer at the time of Independence was KS Thimayya who joined Sandhrust after preparatory training at the Prince of Wales Royal Indian Military College and in due course, was commissioned in 1926. He was first attached to Highland Light Infantry, a Scotish Infantry unit at Bangalore for one year. Later he joined 19 Hyderabad Regiment (Kumaon).

He served with the Battalion in the North West Frontiers. In the beginning of World War II he served with his Battalion in Singapore. He attended Staff College course at Quetta. Thimayya served in Burma during Second Arakan campaign at Maungdaw, Buthidaung and Kangaw areas with his Battalion. He commanded 8/19 Hyderabad Battalion as part of 51 Brigade. It was an All Indian Brigade. All three Battalions were Indian and their commanding officers were also Indian.

8/19 was occupying defense in Arakan in 1944. Opposite 8/19 was a strong Japanese position. They used to fire on the Brigade Sector, harass and cause casualty daily. Finally it was decided to attack and capture the hostile Japanese held hill. Lt Col Thimayya volunteered to attack with his Battalion. But a British battalion was tasked to capture the Japanese post and they failed. Thimayya on his own attacked the Japanese and captured the objective without suffering even a single casualty. The Division Commander appreciated his effort and he was awarded with a DSO.

The Command Team 51 Infantry Brigade - Lt Cols SPP Thorat, LP Sen, Brig Hutton and Lt Col Thimayya DSO

Thimayya was given the command of 39 Infantry Brigade in 26 Division in Burma and he became the first Indian to command a brigade in Buma. Later he was selected to command 268 Brigade in Japan as part of British Commonwealth Force. Back in India in November 1946 he joined the Armed Forces Nationalisation Committee under Sir Gopalaswamy Iyengar. The committee after deliberation decided to retain only a few British senior officers as advisors for a limited period.

Later Thimayya was appointed as Commander of 5 Brigade as part of Boundary Force to maintain law and order during partition in Punjab and Delhi areas. On his recommendation British officers were removed from the Boundary Force. During Independence in 1947, Brigadier Thimayya who was the Commander of 11 Brigade at Jullunder was made commander of the entire Boundary Force. Thimayya was by far the most popular officer of his time. He was well known for his boldness, courage of conviction and luck. (Later he took over 19 Division and saved major part of J&K including Ladakh in 47-48, became Army Commander and COAS.)

JN Chaudhuri was commissioned from Sandhrust in February 1928. Initially he joined North Staffordshire Regiment and later 7 Cavalry in 1929. By 1937 he became a Captain and attended Staff College Course in 1939. He commanded 16 Light Cavalry in Burma in 1944-45. For his gallant and distinguished services he was Mentioned in Dispatches twice. In 1946 he was promoted to the rank of Brigadier and was made in charge of administration in Malaya. He attended the course at Imperial Defense College London in 1947. (Later he headed the Hyderabad operation, became the Adjutant General, Army Commander and COAS.)

JN Chaudhuri

PP Kumaramangalam was commissioned into the Regiment of Artillery in 1933 through Royal Military Academy at Woolwich England. He became a Lieutenant in 1935. He participated in WW II in Libya and was awarded with a Distinguished Service Medal there. He was taken prisoner. He escaped from there but was caught once again. In 1946 he was awarded OBE and was promoted to the rank of Brigadier in 1948. (Later in 1963, he rose to the rank of a Lt Gen and was appointed as Army Commander Eastern Command and Vice Chief before he became the COAS on 8 June 66.)

PP Kumaramangalam

SHFJ Manekshaw was commissioned in December 1934 with the first batch of Indian Officers from the Indian Military Academy Dehradun into the Frontier Regiment. In 1942 in the operation at Sittang River against Japanese in Burma, he led a company counter attack near Pagoda Hill and recaptured the objective. His company suffered heavy casualty and he was seriously injured with seven bullets in his stomach.

Major General David Gowan who was watching the attack, was so impressed by the gallantry and leadership of Maneksha and awarded Military Cross to him by pinning his own MC Medal on the wounded Maneksha. He was so seriously wounded that the General thought he will not recover. But he did recover from his wounds. As captain he attended Staff College Course. Once again in Burma while serving in 14th Army, he was wounded.

After his recovery he was sent to Australia for six months lecture tours to tell about the WW II and Indian Army. In 1947, he joined the Gorkha Rifles and became a Lt Col working at the Army HQ dealing with the problems of partition. (He did not have the opportunity to command an Infantry Battalion but commanded, a brigade, division corps, Army and became the COAS in June 1969 and led the Indian Army successfully in 1971 War with Pakistan. He was the first Indian to be promoted to the rank of Field Marshal in 1972.)

SHFJ Manekshaw

PS Bhagat joined Royal Indian Military College at Dehradun in 1930 and was commissioned from the Indian Military Academy into Royal Bombay Sappers and Miners in July 1939. During the WW II he was posted to 21 Field Company Engineers and was sent to East Africa. 21 Field Company was affiliated to 10 Brigade commanded by Brigadier William Slim (Later Field Marshal) which was engaged in the capture of Fort at Gallabat in north Africa.

Though the Fort was captured, it was lost during the counter attack. While withdrawing from there, 2/Lt Bhagat delayed and prevented the enemy from interfering with his withdrawing brigade by ingeniously destroying a bridge vital to the enemy.

In 1941 before the Battle of Keren in East Africa, Bhagat was awarded a VC for his act of gallantry, his persistent initiative and daring actions against life threatening situation during war while crossing long mine fields. He was promoted to Captain and was chosen to attend the Staff College Course in UK. After WW II he studied engineering in India and UK. On his return to India in 1947, he was promoted as a major.

PS Bhagat

(After 1947, he commanded an engineer regiment, infantry brigade, and was an instructor at Staff College. He worked at the Military Intelligence Branch Army HQ. He coauthored the Henderson Brook-Bhagat report on 1962 war with China. He was the Army Commander of Central and raised Northern Army before he retired and took over the Damodar Valley Corporation).

The inclusion of Indian officers in the British Indian Army took place simultaneously with the freedom movement. Much against the doubts expressed by the outgoing British that the Indians would not be able to provide quality leadership in the independent India; the Indian Army officers proved in all fields' of war that they are as good as any other army officers if not better.

SLIM - THE BRITISH INDIAN ARMY OFFICER

The finest general World War II produced.

- Admiral Earl Mountbatten

Of the three British Field Marshals - Edmund Henry Allenby, Archibald Percival Wavell and William Joseph "Bill" Slim who had the privilege of commanding Indian Troops in the two World Wars, Slim stands out tall as one of the greatest military leader. Unlike the other two, he was truly a British Indian Army Officer who led the Indian Troops from a Company to an Army in war.

While he personally experienced the consequences of a military defeat in Burma under inhuman conditions and ravaged by tropical deceases along with the troops, it was without suffering ignominy. The retreat from Burma was a controlled military withdrawal. The Burma Corps was beaten, but not finished. Slim vowed to avenge the defeat and the sufferings inflicted upon his Corps by the Japanese and he did it.

It was during the First World War that Slim, then a British Army Officer at Gallipoli, saw the Indian Army troops in action for the first time and was impressed by what he saw. There he decided to join British Indian Army and did so in May 1919 as a company commander of 2/7 Gorkha Rifles. Later, he took over the command of the same Battalion.

After commanding the Battalion, he was promoted and became the commander of 10 Indian Brigade in Ethiopia during World War II. He (for the third time in his career) was wounded during advance to Agordat in January 41. On 15 May 1941 he was promoted to Major General and assumed the command of 10 Indian Division in Iraq. During the command of the Division in Iraq, Syria and Lebanon, he was Mentioned in Dispatch twice.

Burma Corps, a weak Corps, comprised 17 Indian Infantry Division and 1 Burma Division was responsible for the internal security of Burma. Against the onslaught of the unexpected attack by the strong Japanese Army, Burma Corps could not stand up and resist the Japanese advance. Slim was promoted to the rank of Lieutenant General and given the command of Burma Corps. It was a great achievement of Slim that he was able to bring back the tattered Burma Corps to the plains of Imphal.

For this magnificent achievement he was made the Commander of the Order of the British Empire (CBE).The men brought back their weapons and evacuated the wounded. They were in rags but retained their unit cohesion and saved India from the Japanese. During the bad days of retreat, Slim ensured that he went through the same hardships that his formation faced. He insisted that the officers will neither eat nor drink or sleep unless the men had eaten and had a place to rest.

Slim was given the command of 15 Corps and was made responsible to conduct offensive operations in Arakan State in Burma. Slim proved that the Japanese were not invincible. He advocated that as and when the Japanese attacked and surrounded the units, the units must stay put and fight organizing all round defense. Their supplies would be air dropped.

The famous Battle of Admin Box was conceived and fought by the 15 Corps successfully by strictly adopting the tactics propounded by Slim. For the first time the Japanese faced an insurmountable Allied Forces in Arakan. The architect of this concept was Lieutenant General Slim whom the troops affectionately called Uncle Slim. No other General even in victory received such affection as was given to Slim by his men.

The 14th Army was raised under Slim with 4, 15 and 33 Corps. This Army had Indians, British and West African Units. American and Chinese troops were also placed under command. With the failure in the battle of Admin Box, the Japanese increased their offensive efforts and crossed the Indian border and knocked at the doors of Imphal and Kohima. This time the troops of 14th Army were not the same who withdrew from Rangoon two years ago after having defeated by the Japanese. Slim had infused vigor in his Army, trained them and provided with required wherewithal to offer a formidable defense at Kohima and Imphal.

Gen Slim the Army Commander

The result was a complete defeat of the hitherto undefeatable Japanese Army. This was the turning point in the War in Burma. Slim's counter-offensive into Central Burma and the Race to Rangoon were classic examples of offensive action and concentration of force which led to success.

Having anticipated the type of terrain and enemy his Army would face in the Central Burma, he modified his units and made them self contained for mobility. The offensive spirit of the 14th Army was so overwhelming that Meiktila and Mandalay were captured well before the scheduled time. Finally Japanese retreated from Burma in July 1945. Thus Slim though suffered defeat initially but finally led his Army to a glorious victory for the Allies.

On 01 July 1945, Slim was promoted to the rank of General. In one of his addresses to the officers he said, "A general's job is simply to make fewer mistakes than the other fellow. I try hard not to make too many mistakes." He further added that "there is no good or bad unit, it is good or bad officers". After he relinquished the command of 14th Army, he was assigned many important appointments including the member of War Council and Commandant of the Staff College. He retired on 11 may 1948.

Field Marshal William Joseph "Bill" Slim
1st Viscount KG, GCB, GCMG, GCVO, GBE, DSO, MC, KStJ

Both India and Pakistan offered him the appointment of C in C of their country. He refused both. The British Government recalled him from the retirement and appointed him as the Chief of the Imperial General Staff (CIGS). Slim thus became the first Indian Army officer to be become CIGS. It was the greatest honour for an Indian Army officer to be appointed as CIGS over a British Field Marshal Montgomery who had laid claim over that coveted appointment. He was made Field Marshal with formal appointment to the Army Council from 1 January 1949 and remained as the CIGS until 1 November 1952.

He became the Governor General of Australia in 1953. In 1968 Bill Slim was invited to the Staff College, Camberley (UK) to give a talk to the Faculty and Students of the College on Leadership. As was customary, after the Talk, Bill was invited to dinner with the Faculty and Students.

The Commandant of the College, Major General John Sharp thought fit to invite the Indian Student attending the course, Major VR Raghavan (Lt Gen Retired, former DGMO and President Center for Security Analysis) to sit next to Bill during the meal. A good student that he was, Raghavan armed himself to face probing questions from Bill about Indian Army and Burma Campaign from the literatures he had procured from the Hyde Park Book Stores. According to Lt Gen Raghavan, Bill was very happy to be seated with an Indian Army officer and chatted with him throughout the duration of the dinner. When Bill asked Major Raghavan as to which was the most interesting battle in Burma, Raghavan promptly answered, it was the Battle of Kohima which was the turning point in Burma Campaign. To this Bill somewhat nostalgic said, ' it was in the Battle of Meiktila I could maneuver the mechanized forces in the plains to our advantage and annihilate the Japanese and commence the Race to Rangoon'.

While Slim was in his death bed, Lord Mountbatten visited him in 1970. Slim recognized him, held his hand and said, "We did it together, old boy" and died.

In contrast to almost every other outstanding commander of the war, Slim was a disarmingly normal human being, possessed of notable self-knowledge. He was without pretension, devoted to his wife, Aileen, their family and the Indian Army. His calm, robust style of leadership and concern for the interests of his men won the admiration of all who served under him.... His blunt honesty, lack of bombast and unwillingness to play courtier did him few favors in the corridors of power. Only his soldiers never wavered in their devotion.

- Max Hastings, Military Historian

Morale is that intangible force which will move a whole group of men to give their last ounce to achieve something without counting the cost to them; that makes them feel they are part of something greater than themselves.

- Slim